Daisy B. Fields is president of Fields Associates, a human resources development and consulting firm in Maryland. She designs and conducts career development training programs tailored to the needs of women in federal government and has conducted similar programs for women in state and local governments as well as in the private sector. She is currently a part-time executive director of The Women's Institute at The American University, Washington, D.C. and is also actively involved in several professional women's organizations.

A WOMAN'S GUIDE TO MOVING UP IN BUSINESS & GOVERNMENT

DAISY B. FIELDS

A SPECTRUM BOOK

Prentice-Hall, Inc., Englewood Cliffs, New Jersey 07632

Library of Congress Cataloging in Publication Data

Fields, Daisy B.
  A woman's guide to moving up in business and government.

  "A Spectrum Book"--T.p. verso.
  Bibliography: p.
  Includes index.
  1. Vocational guidance for women--United States.
2. Women in the civil service--United States. 3. Women
in business--United States. I. Title.
HD6058.F49 1983   331.7'02'024042   83-17634
ISBN 0-13-961813-9
ISBN 0-13-961805-8 (pbk.)

1   2   3   4   5   6   7   8   9   10

Printed in the United States of America

ISBN 0-13-961813-9

ISBN 0-13-961805-8 {PBK.}

Prentice-Hall International, Inc., *London*
Prentice-Hall of Australia Pty. Limited, *Sydney*
Prentice-Hall of Canada Inc., *Toronto*
Prentice-Hall of India Private Limited, *New Delhi*
Prentice-Hall of Japan, Inc., *Tokyo*
Prentice-Hall of Southeast Asia Pte. Ltd., *Singapore*
Whitehall Books Limited, *Wellington, New Zealand*
Editora Prentice-Hall do Brasil Ltda., *Rio de Janeiro*

To Stacy, age three, on whose behalf
I shall continue to chip away at
the barriers to equal opportunity
for women in all aspects of our society.

Contents

Preface

The primary focus of this book is on employment of women in federal civil service. It is the area I know best, having spent nearly three decades in public service.

I also earned my stripes in the business world while attending college at night. I was at various times a salesclerk in the high-fashion salon of a department store, a bookkeeper, and a switchboard operator; and I even tried a stint at being a trainee dietician in a hospital (I quit because I fainted at the sight of blood), before finding my niche in the field of personnel management. So I am familiar with the barriers that impede women's progress to positions of influence and power in the private sector as well.

It is my hope that women in the corporate world, particularly those aspiring to enter that world, will find many of the suggestions and recommendations applicable to them as well.

To protect the identity of individuals who shared their experiences with me, I have used fictitious names.

Although some of the incidents related in this book do not have happy endings, they are not intended to discourage you from seeking federal employment but, rather, to alert you to the signals so you can act accordingly.

As women become more assertive, knowledgeable, and aware of their rights to equal employment opportunity, and begin to exercise these rights, there is no way to go but UP.

Climbing the career ladder is no bed of roses for most women. But armed with appropriate tools—education, experience, ambition, determination, and flexibility—there is no limit to what women can achieve.

In the words of Judge Erastus Culver (1860), "If you want to know, really and sincerely, what woman's sphere is, leave her unhampered and untrammeled, and her own powers will find that sphere. She may make mistakes, and try, as man often does, to do things that she cannot, but the experiment will settle the matter; and nothing can be more absurd than for man, especially a priori, to establish the limits which shall bound woman's sphere, or for woman, as a mere matter of speculation, to debate what her sphere shall be, since the natural laws are revealed, not to speculation, but to action."

Acknowledgments

Throughout the preparation of this book I frequently sought and received information, suggestions, and relevant materials from several women with whom I have maintained a close association since my retirement from federal employment.

I am especially indebted to Florence Perman, Director, Personnel Policy Division, Department of Health and Human Services and former Director of the Federal Women's Program for the Department; and to Carol Harvey, Deputy Director, Federal Women's Program, Office of Personnel Management. Both of these women gave generously of their time and talent whenever I sought their counsel. I am deeply grateful to them.

Thanks also to Rose Thorman, who, until her retirement, was the Federal Women's Program Manager for the Bureau of Mines, Department of the Interior, and who shared with me her views on mentors and networks.

Lisa Carlson, President, Professional Managers Association, formerly coordinator for Executive Development for Women, Office of Personnel Management, was another supportive associate. She scheduled interviews for me with a number of high-level federal women whose comments have been incorporated in this book.

To these women and to the sixteen corporate women, all of whom took the time to complete a lengthy questionnaire in addition to spending hours with me in oral interviews, my gratitude knows no bounds.

I am equally indebted to Diane Weaver, Vice Chair, Maryland Commission for Women, member of the staff of Hagerstown Jr. College, and member, Maryland Advisory Council for Career Education, for permission to include her article on "Career Development and Decision Making," which was published in the Maryland Commission for Women newsletter, February 1982.

Introduction

PART I

To set the tone for this book, I have included the following article entitled *Career Development and Decision Making*, because it offers guidelines to self-awareness, career awareness, and decision making; all vital components to a satisfying career.

Background information on the author, Diane Weaver, appears in the Acknowledgments.

CAREER DEVELOPMENT
AND DECISION MAKING

Work, what we *do*, helps to define us to ourselves, to our families, and to our friends. The decisions we make about work influence the whole of our lives. Yet career decisions are often made haphazardly or in many cases are made before we realize it. Further, at no time have those decisions been more difficult to make. Just as men no longer automatically follow their father's leads, women no longer unthinkingly accept traditional roles set for their lives. Options have dramatically increased for both sexes, and choices already made are being questioned and changed. Job satisfaction and fulfillment through work are becoming the new cliches.

This article attempts to put the issue of career planning into perspective. Although its focus is upon women, almost all of the points made are equally applicable to men. The article presents some of the major elements of career development, outlines briefly a model for career planning, and offers suggestions for further information and assistance.

The last ten years have seen first a trickle and then a torrent of literature and materials related to career preparation, career entry, re-entry, and career changing. Public and private school systems have begun to emphasize career education in the elementary, middle and high schools. Colleges, particularly community colleges, faced with confused, undecided entering students, have added career counseling services to their responsibilities.

The movement toward career education, paralleling women's struggle for equal treatment, has helped many women to learn about and prepare for a greater variety of careers. Yet, the tradition of sex role stereotyping has not by any means died. Consider this typical life story:

By the time a girl enters elementary school, she has logged many hours with "girls' toys," and she has learned about her future role, if not through her parents, then via television. Once in school, with too few exceptions, her teachers and textbooks will reinforce the sex role stereotyping she has already absorbed. Year by year, decisions about her future will be subtly made for her. So it is no wonder that by the time she must choose between algebra and cheerleading, there is no choice. And that one non-decision, preceded by years of unconscious decisions, is a major career choice. Algebra is a career choice screener, a strainer, if you will. Those who do not complete two years of high school algebra are automatically screened out of hundreds of career choices.

With her options collapsing, our "typical" young woman picks a college major, perhaps several different majors. If she manages to hang on and graduate from college, it suddenly hits her: she must find a job. Without planning or foresight, her career path begins its zig-zag, largely thoughtless, course. If she marries and has children, she may become a "re-entry" woman or a "displaced homemaker", who at forty years old wishes to or must set new priorities for her life. The many skills she has learned and used may or may not help her to compete with not only younger job seekers, but her contemporaries as well.

As bleak as this life scenario seems, the life stories of many women are even more frustrating; women who must from an early age support families and cannot afford further education or training face even greater difficulties than college-educated women.

A good career development program that begins in elementary school and continues through formal education and into the workplace can help to reverse the effects of sex role stereotyping. The system that is outlined is being used in varying degrees by schools and businesses and by individuals. It should be kept in mind that this is a summary of a career development system and is not meant to replace a more detailed career planning course or process.

The major components of a career development system are self awareness, and decision making. The system is designed for lifelong use. That is, once learned, it can and should be used frequently, since career development, like physical exercise, is a lifelong process. Activities within each component will be suggested for your use.

Self-Awareness

Certainly before one leaps to make a career decision, she must consider those unique qualities she possesses. The area of self-awareness has in the past been the most neglected element of career planning. Its neglect has in part resulted in compliance that range from job dissatisfaction to burnout.

Self-awareness when applied to career development is not a metaphysical exercise and is not arrived at through meditation. It consists of knowing and stating in a specific way your interests, your skills, your values and your lifestyle preferences.

You might begin by writing your career autobiography, several pages outlining your family history, your childhood dreams and activities, all of your paid and unpaid jobs, your achievements, and your current activities and aspirations. This document can help you pinpoint those interests, skills and values that recur throughout your life.

Interests
Interests are those things you enjoy doing: reading, sewing, keeping a journal, for instance. You have many interests, each on a different level. Write out a list of your interests, including the activities which flow from those interests. Note also how your interests have grown and changed throughout your life.

Skills
Skills are those things you do well. In most cases, people like to do what they do well, so you should find some of the same things on your interest list. Do you organize well? Are you a good speaker? If you have difficulty pinning your skills down, look at your interests and try to analyze them from a skills perspective. For more clues to your skills, ask your friends. Many times friends can help us see more clearly those areas in which we excel. Consider also your achievements. What projects have you completed? What accomplishments are you proud of?

Values
The next step in your self assessment is to consider your personal value system, particularly as it might apply to a work setting. Values are those cherished beliefs we live by, and they have great importance in our working lives. Some of the most common work-related values are independence, prestige, security, monetary rewards, recognition, social contact, achievement and self satisfaction. So you want a high level job and at the same time have a great deal of leisure time? If so, you might be facing a value conflict. Potential value conflicts can be minimized if you have clearly identified your system of values.

Lifestyle
The final element of the self awareness process is a consideration of lifestyle, literally how you wish to live your life and whether or not you have a great deal of flexibility. Are you a city person, or a rural person? What kind

of environment do you prefer for yourself and your family? Are you a money spender or a saver? What place will work occupy in your life?

One of the most important questions about values and lifestyle involves the way you view work. Do you see a job as fulfilling most or all of your needs? Do you see yourself deriving most of your satisfaction from your job? Unless you are willing to give your all *to* a job, you should not count on receiving all *from* your job.

Career Awareness

When your self assessment satisfies you (it will never be complete), you are ready to begin matching your qualities with those required in various careers. You might begin by taking a vocational interest inventory, or by browsing through career reference materials in public libraries, community colleges or community counseling centers. Or you could begin by listing things you might like to do. Research information about the occupations, including education necessary, job duties, salary and advancement opportunities. Match your interests and skills with those occupations which remain on your list. By researching, you will discover other related occupations about which you may not have been aware. Talk to people who do the job you think you'd like to do. How did they become interested in their career? What do they like and dislike about it? What skills does it require? What other fields might they be qualified to enter? For additional information, see the bibliography of publications and resources at the end of this article.

You should begin to find yourself focusing on a few choices which seem to fit your particular qualities and needs. To further explore your career interest, you might volunteer to work in an agency or business in your chosen field, or do more informational interviews in greater depth.

Decision Making

A decision-making procedure of some kind or other is used by everyone, everyday. A systematic process, however, must be employed when alternatives of some importance are being considered. There are several variations of a decision-making process, but most include five steps, briefly summarized below.

1. *Identify the decision to be made.*
   This very important step sounds simple, yet it is sometimes elusive.

Are you choosing from the actual alternatives? Have you narrowed your decision to manageable parts?

2. *Gather information.*
Don't leave anything out. Begin listing possible solutions.

3. *Weigh the alternatives.*
Compare, contrast, assign point values if you like. Look for utility and probability of success. Try to judge risk, possible consequences, and effects on others.

4. *Decide.*
Remember that not to decide is to decide. If you can't decide, go back through the process. Maybe you've forgotten something. If you still can't decide, perhaps you are not quite ready. Relax and let your brain work on the solution. When you do decide, set some goals for yourself. Make sure your goals are attainable, that they are written down, that they include timetables, that they include alternate strategies, and that they reflect your wants and needs.

5. *Review your decision.*
Part of your goal setting strategy should be to look back and evaluate the decision you've made. Was it the right decision for you? If not, you can get over it.

PART II

Worldwide, federal civilian employment, including blue-collar and postal employees, totaled slightly less than 2½ million as of October 31, 1980. This data base will be used throughout the book, primarily because no later statistics are available.

Extensive reductions in federal civilian employment have been occurring since 1981, and will continue at an accelerated pace throughout 1983. It's safe to say that total federal civilian employment by the end of 1983 will likely be somewhat less than 2¼ million. More about that in Chapter 4.

The category of positions with which this book deals is known by the acronym PATCO (Professional, Administrative, Technical, Clerical, and Other). "Other" includes positions in miscellaneous occupations, such as guard, police, fire protection and prevention, U.S. Marshal and correctional officer series, or in various student trainee series.

Our concentration is on professional, administrative, technical, and clerical occupations. In these categories in 1980, men held 1,217,940 of all white-collar positions and women held 767,117 positions.

Figure 1-3 reveals the percentage of women and men in all full-time white-collar occupations throughout the government.

The reader will note that women occupy about 69 percent of positions in the general administration, clerical, and office services category. Not surprising, since tradition has ordained these are the occupations for which women are "best suited."

Many college-educated women hold such jobs, though not through choice. In need of employment and despairing of getting into professions for which they have been trained, they accept clerical jobs, hoping thereby to get a foot in the door that could lead to something better.

In leadership and policy-making positions (grades GS-16 to 18 and Executive Levels) only 3.4 percent are women. The executive suite still is a male preserve, and it is not likely to change in the immediate future.

However, through the efforts of the Equal Employment Opportunity Commission to enforce the laws, and the increasing number of court suits being won by women on the basis of sex discrimination in employment, some of the barriers have begun to crumble.

Since the early 1960s, through my association with organized women's groups in and out of government, I have heard many tales of frustration, anger, and despair resulting from women's futile efforts to move into positions worthy of their talents. Within the last decade, as women have begun to take matters into their own hands by joining women's organizations that provide workshops and seminars on assertive skills, self-development, and career awareness, among others, they have begun to move up in professional and technical positions in the mid-level range, grades GS9 to 12.

Gratifying as this may be, they still have not made the breakthrough into the "feeder" grades, grades 13 to 15, in sufficient numbers to become eligible for supervisory and management jobs. Here the barricades are still up, although a few bolts are loosening. Much work lies ahead before we can overcome the biases that keep women from advancing.

There are no quick solutions to the problem. But with the law on their side, women must continue to demonstrate that they have the stamina, the training, the education, and the determination to advance to their highest potential. They must develop confidence in their own abilities, learn to cope with intimidation and rebuffs, and march determinedly toward their goals.

Let me give you a couple of examples of the kinds of crises women have faced in federal service and what they did about them.

In 1970, armed with a master's degree in journalism and a qualifying rating on an appropriate civil service list, Ellen Brown sought appointment in several federal agencies as a public information specialist (writer). She never made it. In despair, and in keeping with the traditional pattern, she accepted a secretarial job, confident that being "in" would facilitate her transfer to a professional position.

In the course of her employment, several vacancies occurred in the Public Information Office. She applied for every one of them. She was never granted the courtesy of an interview. Each job was filled by a man. Appeals to her supervisor and to the personnel officer for an explanation for her non-selection, and her pleas for an opportunity to demonstrate her knowledge and skills were met with vague excuses.

After two years of frustration with the underuse of her skills and knowledge, she resigned. During the course of processing her resignation papers, the personnel clerk let slip that Ellen's supervisor had *ordered* the personnel officer not to refer her for other positions because she was such a "bright, attractive, and efficient secretary" he couldn't afford to lose her. The personnel officer, playing "footsie" with management, instead of maintaining the integrity of his office, bowed to the manager's request.

Such incidents are not uncommon. Had she been more assertive and sought a mentor in the organization, another woman with whom to share her concerns, perhaps someone could have helped open doors for her. But she was a quiet, conscientious young woman who kept her problems to herself and never challenged "the system." It wasn't until after she had left the agency, not telling anyone where she was going, that we learned of the incident.

My own case was even more ego shattering. For five-and-a-half years I had served as deputy director of personnel in a small federal agency. One day my boss, the director, informed me he was leaving to take another position elsewhere. A few days later the agency head called me to his office to discuss filling the vacancy. He began the conversation with a recitation of my achievements, commending me for the many "innovative contributions" I had made over the years and said he hoped I was not planning to leave the organization. I assured him I had no such intentions. Truth is, after all those accolades, I was sure he was about to offer me the director's job. After all, I thought, who was better qualified? Alas, it was not to be. Instead he asked me to help him find a replacement for Mr. Smith.

Noting my ill-concealed disappointment, he leaned toward me across the desk and said, with a reassuring smile, "I'm sure you understand that it's fine for a woman to be a deputy, but the head of a department really has to be a man."

I hasten to add that this trauma occurred before passage of the Civil Rights Act of 1964, while it was still legal for employers to specify sex preference in hiring.

When I recovered my poise, I responded, "No, Dr. Adams, I do not understand, but if that is your wish, so be it." With that, I bolted out of the chair and beat a hasty retreat to my own office, where I promptly pulled out an application blank and proceeded to look for another job.

In due time I found a replacement for Mr. Smith and gave him my blessings and explained the duties he was expected to perform. Shortly thereafter I landed a job in another agency, which turned out to be one of the most exciting, challenging, and interesting of my entire career in government.

In retrospect, perhaps I should have been grateful to the old chauvinist for giving me the incentive to move onward and upward.

Are you now thinking that if that's how things are, who wants to work for Uncle Sam? Let me assure you, having worked in the public and private sector, if I were starting my career over again, I still would for many reasons choose to work for the federal government. Principal among them is the opportunity to find a job in almost any field you care to enter, although admittedly in some occupations very few are hired. There is increasing evidence that agencies are responding to the legal mandate to provide more opportunities for women, especially in areas in which women are grossly underrepresented. Flexible working hours are becoming the order of the day—a boon to women with family responsibilities.

The government has generous sick and vacation leave policies—another boon to parents of young children. There are health and life insurance programs; periodic salary increases (subject to satisfactory job performance); and a retirement system considered one of the best in the world. If you transfer from one government agency to another, no matter how long you have been in a particular one, your retirement pension rights move along with you without interruption.

Women now are eligible for positions that previously bore a "for men only" label. For example, until 1971, women were not permitted to carry firearms, which excluded them from law enforcement jobs. When the restriction was finally lifted, women were actively recruited for the Secret Service, the Marshals Service, the Drug Enforcement Administration, the Bureau of Prisons, and the Federal Bureau of Investigation, among other agencies.

One woman, a Border Patrol Agent responsible for preventing illegal entry into the United States, says of her work, "I love the job. There's no greater sense of accomplishment than when you can start out in a tiny border station . . . and track 'a set of signs' (marks or traces of a person) right up to apprehension."

This is not to suggest that women are being greeted with open arms in this male bastion, but the bright ones know how to deal with situations that arise and are "making it" despite the opposition. As more women enter these occupations and prove they do just as well as men, they will gain greater acceptance, and, who knows, maybe attitudes will change and the stereotype of "woman's role" will become a matter of history.

At best, the world of work is a jungle, no matter what the occupation. Ask anyone who has been in it for a while, striving to climb the ladder of success, in the public or the private sector. But we learn to tread lightly through the underbrush of the jungle, carefully avoiding the snakes, as we seek an open field and room to breathe. It is there. Women must develop the techniques men have used so effectively: How to Play the Game; Understanding Office Politics; Cultivating the "Right" People; and Finding a Mentor.

For all women, those seeking career advancement and college students about to take their first step into the "jungle," it is important to know how the system works; how to prepare for the job you want; where the best job opportunities may be; how to get the particular job you want; and, finally, once you are "in" the system, how to make it work for you.

That is the purpose of this book.

"Your promotion will give you enormous new responsibilities, extensive authority, a much larger workload, and a slight increase in salary."

FEDERAL WORKER PORTRAIT*

Mr. Ford of Michigan. Mr. Speaker, we all carry in our minds stereotypes of groups in our society. They often little resemble reality.

Take the workers in the Federal civilian work force. It is probably true that this very title conjures up in the American mind an image of paper shufflers wearing green eye shades at their desks in obscure Washington offices. It is probably true as well that these nondescript figures are regarded as overpaid, underworked and that they multiply geometrically.

Sadly, this picture is terribly distorted. It squares not at all with the way things really are.

The people who are lumped together, sometimes derisively, as Government workers are doctors, lawyers, electricians, brick masons, accountants, shipbuilders, deep sea divers, oceanographers, scientists, typists, mechanics, secretaries, architects, librarians, teachers, mailmen, and so forth.

In short, they are the people who live next door. The only difference is that they do not work for General Motors, United States Steel, Prudential Life Insurance, the local supermarket or the neighborhood automobile dealership. On the average they earn about $20,000 a year, which closely parallels the median family income in the United States. They raise about the same number of children as other Americans, have home mortgages and automobile payments and other expenses like the family down the block.

At last count there were 2,907,259 men and women working full time for the Federal Government, not including the military.

And to put to rest the notion that these are mostly bureaucrats in musty Washington offices, consider this:

Only 7.64 percent of all Federal employees work in the District of Columbia. Actually there are more Federal workers in the State of California than any place else in America—nearly 300,000 of them for a total of 10.65 percent of the total Federal workforce. Michigan has 53,350; New York 166,194; Texas 148,022; Illinois 101,687; Ohio 89,444; Georgia 75,941; Alabama 59,857; Pennsylvania 128,018.

It is disheartening to hear, as we do these days, blanket condemnations of Federal Government workers. All too frequently they are the brunt of

*Statement by Congressman William D. Ford (Mich.), *Congressional Record* (March 11, 1981).

jokes as they are portrayed as free loaders at the public trough. Nothing could be farther from the truth.

The truth is that if we did not have Federal workers spread across the face of this land we would have to invent them.

They build and repair our Navy's ships. They deliver our mail. They guide our commercial airliners in and out of crowded airways. Every day they are developing new treatment and cures for disease. They make sure that the food we eat is safe. They make possible the flow of commerce. Without them our kind of society could not survive.

The farmers in America would find their lives a good deal more difficult without county agricultural agents who test their soils, recommend rotation practices and perform countless other services. Of the 93,843 employees in the Department of Agriculture, very few are necessary paper shufflers in Washington. Mostly they work near the farm lands in occupations ranging from soil conservationists to veterinarians. For the record, there are 3,200 people working for the Federal Government in the field of veterinary medical science. Among other things, they guarantee that our food supplies are not contaminated by disease.

The next time you are tempted to think of these public servants as pencil pushers, remember that mathematicians and physicists employed by the Federal Government launch our space vehicles. There are 9,834 persons employed in the physical sciences. Remember, too that it is the investigators at the FBI and lawyers at the Justice Department—in cities across America—who protect our laws and prosecute those who violate them. This is

*Congressional Record, March 11, 1981

a nation of laws populated by more than 200 million citizens. The figure of 20,882 persons working in legal and kindred employment hardly sounds unreasonable.

It is true that the largest single concentration of white-collar workers is in Washington. But this is hardly surprising since Washington houses the headquarters for most departments and agencies.

We hear a lot about waste and inefficiency in the Federal Government. Of course there is some. It would indeed be surprising if there were not. We will find some waste and inefficiency in the best managed American corporations. It is unavoidable in any undertaking—from the lowest household to the largest corporation. The difference is that Government is always under close scrutiny because it spends the public's money. Reporters do not look for waste at General Motors, United States Steel, IBM, or Texas Instruments, even though the public pays for waste and inefficiency in the business and industrial community through higher prices.

Government does have a special obligation to insure that the people's money is spent wisely. Waste and fraud should be pursued diligently. Where it is found it should be cut out. But this should be done surgically, not with a meat ax. In trimming the fat we must take care not to mutilate the steak.

It has taken two centuries to build the machine that is our Federal work force. The vast majority of workers are in their jobs because there is indispensable work to be done to keep the Nation operating. There is no question that unneeded jobs should be eliminated, that unnecessary workers be let go and procedures streamlined wherever possible. But we should avoid a helter-skelter approach that threatens, in the name of economy, the vital work that must be done.

When we set out to eliminate jobs, we must know precisely what we are doing. Before we act we must have a good idea of the consequences. Do we have too many food inspectors, too many customs officials, too many social security clerks, too many doctors at the National Institutes of Health, too many county agricultural agents, or too many air traffic controllers?

Just these few examples provide an insight into the importance of Federal workers to our daily living. Without them we could not travel safely. We could not trust the very food we eat. So many of the services on which we depend would not be there without the Federal worker.

We have become a very complex society. It requires considerable expertise to keep it operating. There are those of us old enough to remember the Model-T Ford. Pop and the boys could usually keep it running with a few inexpensive parts that were relatively easy to install. Anyone who has looked under the hood of an automobile today understands that keeping it on the road is no job for the average backyard mechanic. And what has happened to the automobile is really a microcosm of what has happened to our society.

This means a lot of people. But consider this: The total number of full-time Federal workers has remained virtually unchanged since 1967 and the ratio per 1,000 population has declined from 16.3 to 12.4 since 1952.

Planning
Ahead

I doubt that any enlightened American woman today still clings to the myth of the knight in shining armor carrying her off to an ivy-covered cottage to live happily ever after. The statistics on divorce, separation, and widowhood make it clearly evident that such notions belong to an earlier century.

Evidence is conclusive that women increasingly are pursuing higher education and the more educated a woman becomes, the more likely she is to seek paid employment, regardless of her marital status.

What better evidence than the fact that today 50 percent of all women are in the labor force and, according to a recent study, by 1990 the projection is for 57 percent of all women to be gainfully employed.

If for no other reason than economic necessity or economic security, it makes sense to prepare yourself with marketable skills in this unpredictable world with its rapidly changing technological advances.

Contrary to common belief, most government jobs are *not* in Washington D. C. As a matter of fact, only 14 percent of federal white-collar employees are located in the nation's capital; 84 percent are spread across the nation, and a little over 2 percent are overseas in foreign countries and in United States territories.

The largest single employer is the Department of Defense, the bread-and-butter source for 29 percent (575,846) federal employees, followed by the Postal Service with 24.3 percent (482,701). Other agencies with large numbers of employees in the District of Columbia and in many field establishments across the United States are the Veterans Administration, 8.2 percent (162,000); the Department of Health and Human Services, 6.7 percent (127,749); Treasury, 5.8 percent (111,633); and the Department of Agriculture, 4.5 percent (92,197). The remaining agencies employ 21.8 percent nationwide.

The Office of Personnel Management (formerly U.S. Civil Service Commission) publishes a pamphlet entitled "Graduate to Government: The Employment Picture for College Graduates." It is directed at recent college graduates interested in federal employment and contains, among such items as how to apply for a job, an occupational survey of annual career-entry hires, including those areas offering best employment opportunities.

Table 1-1 gives a few examples from a recent edition.

TABLE 1-1.

Occupations	Academic Majors	Average Annual Openings	Employment Prospects and Trends
Accountants, Auditors	Accounting	1500	Good opportunities expected for high-quality applicants but competition is keen. Serious candidates should apply well in advance of graduation date. Excellent promotion and long-range career opportunities.
Administrative Officers/ Assistants	All majors	30–40	High competitive; applicants with management courses or majors in business or public administration may have a slight edge for some positions.

TABLE 1-1. (continued)

Occupations	Academic Majors	Average Annual Openings	Employment Prospects and Trends
Claims Examiners	All majors	1260	Very good opportunities for employment. Major employers are Social Security Administration and Veterans Administration.
Economists	Economics	450	Excellent opportunities in labor, agriculture, industry econometrics, international economics, natural resources, finance and transportation. Positions are available nationwide, but demand is greatest in Washington, D. C.
Medical Technologists	Medical Technology, Chemistry	650	Opportunities are very good in most geographic locations. Applicants willing to work in locations outside of metro areas have excellent prospects.
Engineers Civil	Engineering	650	Good opportunities, especially in the Southwest and Mid-Atlantic.
Electronic/ Electrical	Engineering	950	Current supply/demand is strongly favorable to applicants and expected to continue.
Writers and Editors	All majors	70	Very competitive. Interested applicants greatly outnumber openings.

Don't be discouraged by the fact that there seem to be so few vacancies. Remember, these are averages as of a particular date. Some agencies, in some geographic locations, periodically experience a rash of openings as people retire, got promoted to other jobs, or transfer elsewhere. Not all vacancies are brought to the attention of the Office of Personnel Management.

All departments and agencies of government publish booklets or pamphlets about their mission and the specific work performed by their employees. Many of these are illustrated with actual photographs of employees engaged in a wide variety of occupations. It is an education in itself just to read them. They are living proof of how dependent the nation is on the civil service work force for life, liberty, and the pursuit of happiness.

Many of these pamphlets also contain information about the kinds of career opportunities available. Some departments publish separate pamphlets or booklets on career opportunities. It is well to write and ask for both.

To give you an idea, here are some excerpts from a few publications:

"Women in the Defense Mapping Agency." An attractive little flyer featuring women at work in a variety of occupations. It states, in part, " . . . there are women cartographers . . . security specialists, librarians, computer programmers and analysts, photographers and illustrators, physical scientists and geodesists, mathematicians, editors, accountants, budget analysts, and many others."

The Department of Agriculture issues a publication called "Careers in the Food and Nutrition Service." It outlines specific opportunities in three areas: program administration, management, and nutrition, as well as opportunities for typists and stenographers, and briefly sketches what is entailed in the different kinds of jobs within each major category.

Jobs in the Food and Nutrition Service of the Department of Agriculture are not limited to Washington, D. C. In fact their employees are located in seven regional offices and in field offices across the country.

The Department of Housing and Urban Development (HUD) has a fact sheet called "Don't Let Your Future Get Away—HUD College Co-op Program Fact Sheet." Eligible participants in this work-study program may look forward to positions in the areas of accounting, housing, planning, engineering, and management.

The United States Army Corps of Engineers publishes a most attractive, colorful booklet called, simply, "Careers." The Corps employs 45,000 civilians working in every state in the nation and in more than ten nations overseas. Typically, as in every federal agency, or in any private corporation for that matter, the Corps employs legal, administrative, technical, and financial management personnel. But it specifically seeks qualified people in a variety of disciplines, among them: accountants, agronomists, architects, attorneys, auditors, biologists, computer specialists, ecologists, economists, engineers, foresters, geologists, hydrologists, landscape architects, mathematicians, physicists, realty specialists, recreation specialists, social scientists, sociologists, and urban planners.

Similarly, the Environmental Protection Agency (EPA) has a pamphlet called "Career Choices." In addition to describing the mission of the agency, it lists a variety of careers, with a brief description of the functions in each category and the specific educational requirements. Typical job titles in the area of environmental technology and education include environmental educators, environmental engineers, environmental health services, environmental planners, and natural-resource managers. In the area of Environmental Science and Research are life scientists, physical scientists, and social and behavioral scientists.

At the end of Chapter 2 you will find addresses for all Personnel Offices of the Executive Departments and Independent Agencies. If there is one you would like to work for, write and request a copy of the booklet describing the organization.

Certain occupations, not generally listed in these booklets, are common to all government agencies, as they are in most corporations in the private sector. These include personnel technicians and specialists, accountants and auditors, general administrative and clerical personnel, and attorneys.

The number employed in each category naturally depends upon the size of the organization, the number of field establishments, and proposed expansions of programs.

Except for top management officials, most of whom are political appointees, all hiring is done locally by the respective field office of a department or agency. For example, if you want to work for the National Aeronautics and Space Administration in Houston, Texas, you should apply directly to the Johnson Space Center, Houston, Texas.

There are a few occupations that offer little prospect for employment in federal civil service. One, for example, is anthropology. If you have a burning desire to spend your working life as an anthropologist for Uncle Sam, forget it! A total of fifty-nine anthropologists (forty-nine men, ten women) work for the federal government. They are employed in national parks, museums, the Bureau of Indian Affairs, and a few in technical aid programs.

On the other hand, if your education and training are in a health-related field, you can almost write your own ticket.

For example, the Veterans Administration, with more than 100 hospitals throughout the nation, is the largest single employer of health professionals. Others include Health Services Administration; Food and Drug Administration; Alcohol, Drug Abuse and Mental Health Administration; and the Public Health Service, all in the Department of Health and Human Services (formerly Department of Health, Education and Welfare).

The Air Force, the Department of Agriculture and ACTION also employ health professionals.

The variety of jobs in these agencies include physicians, dentists, industrial hygienists, physical and occupational therapists, nurses, physicians' assistants, medical records librarians, medical technologists, and medical technicians.

Opportunities also are excellent for engineers, physical scientists, and mathematicians—fields in which all too few women specialize.

Under the strengthened provisions of the Civil Service Reform Act of 1978, requiring stricter compliance with equal opportunity and affirmative action laws and regulations, it is anticipated agencies will make a greater effort to recruit women and minorities. Despite these legislative mandates, however, women still are not welcomed with open arms in these male-dominated professions. But those who make it and give their all to the job soon are accepted into the "fraternity."

The sooner more women apply for these occupations, the sooner more will be hired and recognized for their abilities. Only by sheer numbers will we begin to erase the sex-role stereotypes defined as "women's work."

Engineering has many specialties and it is important to know which ones are in demand and where. Women with demonstrated aptitude and interest in these fields can make significant strides.

The Department of the Navy uses engineers in such specialties as petroleum, electronic, mechanical, nuclear, and electrical and naval architects.

The Department of Energy offers similar opportunities, plus chemical, electronic, and general engineers.

Agricultural engineers are sought by the Department of Agriculture. The National Aeronautics and Space Administration seeks mechanical, electronic, aerospace, and general engineers. The Environmental Protection Agency uses similar types.

Biomedical, safety, and electrical engineers are recruited for the Veterans Administration. The Internal Revenue Service hires electrical, industrial, and mechanical engineers. (And you thought all they did was collect taxes!)

The Department of Commerce hires architects and ceramic engineers, as well as all the other types mentioned previously.

This is but a fraction of the areas employing engineers. For women with aptitude and interest in this field, the government can be a good source for a satisfying career.

While overall federal employment will be substantially curtailed in 1982-1983, the demand for engineers with degrees at the bachelor's and master's levels is expected to increase.

According to the Engineering Manpower Commission, women comprised a record high of 10.4 percent of engineering graduates at the baccalaureate level, 6.9 percent at the master's level, and 3.2 percent at the doctoral level. In actual numbers, of 62,935 graduates from engineering schools in 1980–81 with BS degrees, 6,557 were women.

Slowly, slowly, some of the barriers that kept women out of engineering schools are beginning to crumble.

I'm reminded of an incident that occurred several years ago. I was conducting a workshop for a group of engineers, managers of a major oil company, regarding their legal responsibilities for extending equal employment opportunities to women and complying with affirmative action guidelines. One of the men (naturally, all were men) spoke up and said it was impossible to hire women for the kind of work done at a refinery. When I asked why, he responded that no woman would be willing to climb up on an oil storage tank to "check things out." I pursued the matter by asking him how he knew that. The reply was he "just knew" women were afraid to climb heights and certainly could not do so in their miniskirts. As you can well imagine, that remark generated a huge round of knee-slapping guffaws from the entire group.

Following up, I asked if he ever thought of providing women with coveralls, such as most of the men wear, or to allow them to wear slacks. He shook his head and assured me women wouldn't wear such "unfeminine" attire. After further questioning, he admitted no woman had even been offered the opportunity to try it because, based on tradition, it "just wasn't a job for a woman."

Refusing to let the matter rest, I challenged his memory regarding the work women did during World War II, the "Rosie the Riveters," who built aircraft and performed myriad tasks in many industries that had always been performed by men. The answer was, "Oh, that's different, there was a shortage of men at the time!"

Such are the traditional attitudes and behaviors that have created and maintained the barriers to women's access to "men's work." Knowing the prevalence of such attitudes and reluctance to change the system, women have avoided careers in these nontraditional occupations, thereby effectively excluding themselves from a variety of well-paying occupations.

If ever there was a time for women to demonstrate that intellectually they are equal to (and in many cases superior to) the tasks reserved for men, that time is now. The law is on their side and the courts increasingly are sustaining suits brought by women fighting employment discrimination.

Other fields in which recruitment needs are increasing include the physical sciences and mathematics. Best opportunities lie in the fields of chemistry, cartography, geology, hydrology, and physics. Mathematicians with a background in statistics or operations research stand a good chance for employment in a number of agencies. Here too, those with advanced degrees or several years experience are preferred to those with bachelor's degrees only.

The need for accountants and auditors has grown appreciably in the past year. Among the agencies seeking such specialists are the Internal Revenue Service; Departments of Energy, Navy, and Labor; Veterans Administration; Department of Agriculture; Housing and Urban Development; General Accounting Office; Health and Human Services; and the General Service Administration. Many of the jobs are in field and regional offices as well as in Washington, D. C.

Computer specialists, particularly programmers and analysts, will find better opportunities in Washington, D. C. then elsewhere in the country.

Economists, particularly specialists in such fields as labor, finance, international economics, agriculture, econometrics, industry, material resources, or transportation will find the welcome mat in many departments and agencies.

This list is by no means all-inclusive. It is intended to inform you about some of the governmentwide recruitment activities; which agencies actually are hiring, and where the jobs are geographically located.

If you are now in college, it should help you plan a curriculum. If you are in the workforce, it may be of help in redesigning your career aspirations.

Before you apply for a civil service examination, however, you should decide where you want to work, geographically, and how flexible you are willing to be about accepting employment in a part of the United States other than where you currently reside. If you are mobile and willing to accept employment wherever offered, you increase your chances for hire a hundredfold.

The Office of Personnel Management publishes a monthly bulletin called "Trends in Federal Hiring," which is sent to college placement officers. If you are a college student, you should check with your placement office from time to time to ascertain what's new in the federal job market. Needs change frequently. Check often.

The Job Information Centers of the Office of Personnel Management, located in principal cities across the nation, can provide you with a list of current civil service examination announcements that indicate the qualification requirements for each announced examination with instructions on how to apply. It is safe to assume that if an examination is announced, there are jobs to be filled. [List of Federal Job Information Centers (FJICs) appears at the end of Chapter 2.]

We have primarily discussed in this chapter what my dictionary calls the "learned professions." But it also defines a professional as one "engaged in an activity as a means of livelihood or for gain." So, a word for those careerists in other fields.

For high school graduates with no college training and no relevant work experience, clerical and secretarial positions are about the most they can reasonably expect to find. In these occupations opportunities for advancement are rather limited. However, such employees who supplement their experience and education with additional and perhaps specialized courses relevant to the organizations in which they work, may find avenues to progress to higher levels. Much depends upon the individual's initiative and motivation plus support and cooperation from supervisors.

Today the emphasis is on hiring candidates with degrees in business administration, especially those with a Master of Business Administration (MBA), for all kinds of administrative and management positions. With such credentials, career advancement has been remarkably fast for many women.

For the college graduate with a qualifying degree for one of the "learned professions" I have a word of advice. Never admit you can type. Managers are delighted to hire college graduates for secretarial jobs (creating tough competition for the high school graduate).

Too often women who find the going rough in trying to break into their professional fields rationalize that by accepting a secretarial job, the transition to a professional job in the same agency will be easier. As you gathered from the Introduction, "It ain't necessarily so."

In his book, *What Color is Your Parachute?* Richard Bolles put it very succinctly: "The one thing that the job-hunt system in this country does, and does exceedingly well, is scaring people to the point where they are more than willing to lower their self-esteem and hence their expectations as to what they will settle for."

Don't settle for less than you know you are worth. Armed with a marketable skill, have confidence in your ability and pursue your goal. With persistence, patience, and determination you will break into the field for which you trained and find it was worth waiting for.

CHARACTERISTICS OF FEDERAL CIVILIAN WHITE-COLLAR EMPLOYEES

Major Geographic Areas

Figure 1-1 illustrates the distribution of the full-time white-collar employees in the federal civilian work force by major geographic area. A large majority (83.6 percent) of the 1,985,057 white-collar employees worked in the United States outside of the Washington, D. C. Standard Metropolitan Statistical Area (SMSA); 14.1 percent worked in the Washington, D. C. SMSA. The remaining 2.3 percent of the federal white-collar employees worked overseas.

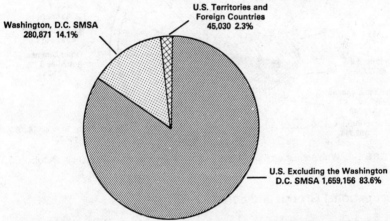

FIGURE 1-1. White-collar employment by major geographic area, October 31, 1980.

Departments and Agencies

The Department of Defense (DOD) employed 575,846 white-collar workers, 29.0 percent of the total federal white-collar work force. Within DOD, Army employed 224,355 white-collar workers, followed by Navy (157,627), Air Force (131,840), Defense Logistics Agency (34,894), and all other Defense components (27,130).

The U.S. Postal Service (USPS) had the second largest concentration (24.3 percent of the total) of white-collar personnel, 482,701 employees, including 451,537 workers in occupations unique to the Postal Service. Together, DOD and USPS employed more than half of all Federal white-collar workers. The Veterans Administration (162,714), Health and Human Services (127,749), Treasury (111,633), and Agriculture (92,197) together employed a quarter (24.9 percent) of the white-collar work force. All other federal departments and agencies employed the remaining 21.8 percent of the white-collar work force. Figure 1-2 presents the distribution of white-collar employment by agency and department.

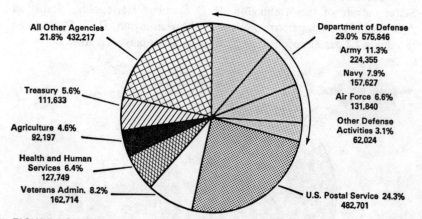

FIGURE 1-2. White-collar employment by department and selected agency, October 31, 1980.

Occupational Groups and Series

The nonpostal occupational series with the greatest number of workers as of October 1980 was Miscellaneous Administration and Programs (series 301) with 93,234 employees. Table 1-2 consists of 1979 and 1980 employment data for the ten largest nonpostal white-collar occupational series.

Employment Trends

The number of full-time white-collar employees in the Federal civilian work force increased by 7,085 (0.4 percent) between October 31, 1979 and October 31, 1980. The largest increase occurred in the Medical, Hospital, Dental, and Public Health group, which gained 7,526 employees (+6.0 percent). The largest decrease took place in the General Administrative, Clerical, and Of-

TABLE 1-2. White-Collar Employment in the Ten Largest Occupations, October 31, 1979 and 1980*

Title	Series	1979 Employment	1980 Employment
Mis. Administration and Programs	301	136,878	93,234**
Secretary	318	65,281	79,470
Clerk-Typist	322	67,235	66,397
Nurse	610	34,830	36,010
Nursing Assistant	621	35,458	35,630
Mis. Clerk and Assistant	303	4,157	34,570**
Supply Clerical and Technician	2005	30,520	30,699
Computer Specialist	334	27,504	28,840
Air Traffic Controller	2152	28,069	27,609
Engineering Technician	802	25,755	26,210

*Excludes occupational series in the Postal Operations Group (2300)

**Occupational series 301 was redefined, and many employees who were in that category in 1979 were reclassified into other series in the General Administrative, Clerical, and Office Services occupational group, particularly into series 303, Miscellaneous Clerk and Assistant.

fice Services group, which declined by 9,573 employees (−2.1 percent). The largest proportional decrease occurred in the Copyright, Patent, and Trademark group (−5.5 percent).

The large increase in the number of employees in the Unspecified group is attributable to the reclassification of approximately 3,000 employees by the General Accounting Office to an occupational series that had not yet been established within OPM's Central Personnel Data File system.

Table 1-4 contains employment data for the period 1968-1980. The number of white-collar workers increased from 1,963,870 in 1968 to 1,992,410 in 1972. Employment then declined in 1973 to 1,893,575. Growth resumed in 1974, was interrupted in 1977, and culminated in a peak of 1,995,129 in 1978. The decline between 1978 and 1979 was reversed in 1980.

During the period 1968-1980, the Social Services, Psychology, and Welfare group grew by 26,736 employees (+78.9 percent). The Legal and Kindred group increased 25,141 (+54.9 percent), and the Medical, Hospital, Dental, and Public Health group rose 37,964 (+40.3 percent). The greatest decrease in full-time positions occurred in Postal Operations, which declined from 585,838 in 1968 to 451,537 in 1980 (−134,301 or −22.9 percent). However, approximately 86,000 full-time employees were reclassified to part-time status between October 1972 and October 1973. The supply group decreased by 26,310 (−31.8 percent), and Equipment, Facilities, and Service declined by 5,780 (−23.3 percent).

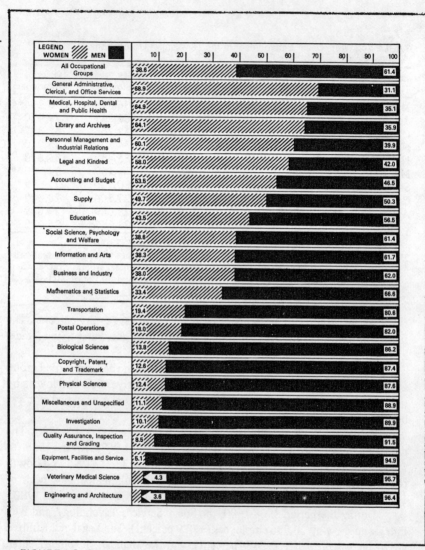

LEGEND WOMEN ▨ MEN ▓	10	20	30	40	50	60	70	80	90	100
All Occupational Groups	38.6									61.4
General Administrative, Clerical, and Office Services	68.9									31.1
Medical, Hospital, Dental and Public Health	64.9									35.1
Library and Archives	64.1									35.9
Personnel Management and Industrial Relations	60.1									39.9
Legal and Kindred	58.0									42.0
Accounting and Budget	53.5									46.5
Supply	49.7									50.3
Education	43.5									56.5
Social Science, Psychology and Welfare	38.6									61.4
Information and Arts	38.3									61.7
Business and Industry	38.0									62.0
Mathematics and Statistics	33.4									66.6
Transportation	19.4									80.6
Postal Operations	18.0									82.0
Biological Sciences	13.8									86.2
Copyright, Patent, and Trademark	12.6									87.4
Physical Sciences	12.4									87.6
Miscellaneous and Unspecified	11.1									88.9
Investigation	10.1									89.9
Quality Assurance, Inspection and Grading	8.5									91.5
Equipment, Facilities and Service	5.1									94.9
Veterinary Medical Science	4.3									95.7
Engineering and Architecture	3.6									96.4

FIGURE 1-3. Distribution of full-time white collar employment by sex within occupational group, October 31, 1980.

LEGEND		AVERAGE ANNUAL SALARY
WOMEN ‖‖‖‖‖‖		
MEN ▬▬▬		(scale: $1000 to $42000)

Occupational Group	Women	Men
Total Full-Time White Collar Employees	16,713	24,437
Postal Operations	18,195	18,843
General Administrative, Clerical, Office Services	14,716	26,373
Engineering and Architecture	18,117	30,098
Accounting and Budget	16,606	26,481
Medical, Hospital, Dental, Public Health	17,811	24,323
Business and Industry	18,337	27,780
Supply	15,596	20,794
Legal and Kindred	18,145	30,740
Miscellaneous	16,256	18,304
Social Science, Psychology, Welfare	23,437	29,890
Biological Sciences	16,630	23,152
Investigation	19,119	27,628
Personnel Management, Industrial Relations	18,278	28,544
Transportation	16,968	30,917
Physical Sciences	21,328	30,609
Education	17,384	24,095
Information and Arts	20,201	27,147
Quality Assurance, Inspection, Grading	17,277	23,631
Equipment, Facilities, Service	19,003	26,829
Mathematics and Statistics	20,801	33,148
Library and Archives	19,992	23,964
Unspecified	22,068	31,649
Veterinary Medical Science	24,379	30,118
Copyright, Patent, Trademark	29,804	41,747

FIGURE 1-4. Average annual salaries of white collar employees by occupational group and sex, October 31, 1980.

TABLE 1-3. Employment and Average Salaries of White-Collar Employees by PATCO Category and Sex, All Areas, October 31, 1980

	TOTAL		MEN		WOMEN	
	Employment	Average Salary	Employment	Average Salary	Employment	Average Salary
Total	1,985,057	$21,452	1,217,940	$24,437	767,117	$16,713
Professional	326,613	30,899	248,694	33,283	77,919	23,289
Administrative	433,281	28,256	320,150	29,995	113,131	23,334
Technical	359,231	18,153	203,266	19,889	155,965	15,891
Clerical	818,370	15,800	402,733	17,650	415,637	14,009
Other	42,242	15,148	38,841	15,388	3,401	12,405
Unspecified[1]	5,320	29,730	4,256	31,649	1,064	22,058

[1] No PATCO Codes can be assigned to employees with unspecified occupation series codes.

15

TABLE 1-4. Trend of Full-Time Civilian White-Collar Employment by Occupational Group, All Areas, as of October 31, 1968-October 31, 1980 (Excludes Foreign Nationals Employed Overseas)

Occupational Group	1968	1970	1972	1973	1974
Total	1,963,870	1,981,722	1,992,410	1,893,575	1,957,252
Miscellaneous occupations	40,190	42,169	46,614	46,373	49,018
Social Science, Psychology and Welfare	33,870	34,219	37,838	41,374	44,956
Personnel Management and Industrial Relations	39,276	40,411	39,808	40,102	41,810
General Administrative, Clerical and Office Services	452,716	449,057	463,902	459,912	473,725
Biological Sciences	40,900	41,531	44,881	43,557	44,476
Accounting and Budget	114,439	113,247	114,751	114,712	118,355
Medical, Hospital, Dental and Public Health	94,169	93,663	105,661	106,369	108,968
Veterinary Medical Science	2,398	2,346	2,353	2,317	2,287
Engineering and Architecture	147,374	148,755	152,404	147,858	146,490
Legal and Kindred	45,777	47,779	44,784	48,024	55,378
Information and Arts	20,380	19,573	19,758	19,296	19,809
Business and Industry	55,284	64,491	65,726	64,755	67,071
Copyright, Patent and Trademark	1,812	1,772	1,728	1,735	1,666
Physical Sciences	43,425	42,967	41,875	40,826	41,025
Library and Archives	8,425	8,496	8,587	8,512	8,892
Mathematics and Statistics	15,575	13,997	14,659	14,176	13,805
Equipment, Facilities, and Service	20,402	18,163	17,087	15,701	15,064
Education	26,614	29,251	29,815	26,579	26,284
Investigation	34,983	38,935	45,868	44,802	45,426
Quality Assurance, Inspection, and Grading[B]	21,387	21,395	19,345	18,834	18,643
Supply	82,625	72,121	66,988	63,608	62,118
Transportation	36,011	42,572	41,165	41,458	42,124
Postal Operations	585,838	594,812	566,396	478,571	498,540
Unspecified[C]	–	–	417	4,124	11,322

[A]U.S. Postal Service figures reflect work force status as of February, 1978.

[B]Formerly titled "Commodity Quality Control, Inspection, and Grading Group," was retitled and redefined effective June, 1970.

1975	1976	1977	1978A	1979	1980	Change 1979-80	Percent Change 1979-80
1,975,745	1,981,163	1,977,848	1,995,129	1,977,972	1,985,057	+7,085	+ 0.4
49,147	50,056	51,758	53,514	53,122	54,067	+ 945	+ 1.8
48,201	53,109	55,719	58,166	59,380	60,606	+1,226	+ 2.1
43,830	44,359	45,660	47,231	47,402	48,464	+1,062	+ 1.8
472,157	471,695	469,169	466,434	458,242	448,669	−9,573	− 2.1
45,615	46,163	49,495	52,313	50,235	51,339	+1,304	+ 2.6
119,463	121,625	124,159	125,950	124,402	125,254	+ 852	+ 0.7
117,409	120,499	120,605	123,088	124,607	132,133	+7,526	+ 6.0
2,828	3,117	3,159	3,200	2,998	2,918	− 80	− 2.7
151,560	151,305	152,306	154,176	152,663	153,772	+1,109	+ 0.7
58,262	64,321	66,581	67,678	67,934	70,918	+2,984	+ 4.4
20,358	20,525	20,584	20,882	20,839	21,278	+ 439	+ 2.1
69,332	69,027	70,302	72,022	73,860	75,889	+2,029	+ 2.7
1,641	1,488	1,640	1,669	1,587	1,499	− 88	− 5.5
41,643	41,746	41,999	42,957	43,063	43,763	+ 700	+ 1.6
9,173	9,673	9,789	9,834	9,673	9,753	+ 80	+ 0.8
14,226	14,586	14,415	14,792	14,776	14,977	+ 201	+ 1.4
14,690	14,047	14,374	14,403	14,622	14,833	+ 211	+ 1.4
28,160	28,656	28,606	28,599	28,924	29,000	+ 76	+ 0.3
45,206	46,547	47,496	48,806	48,983	48,996	+ 13	+ 0.03
18,748	18,721	18,732	18,877	18,965	18,689	− 276	− 1.5
62,390	59,958	59,049	57,230	56,444	56,315	− 129	− 0.2
43,509	43,699	43,830	44,404	44,974	44,868	− 106	− 0.2
489,638	469,572	461,109	465,580	457,923	451,537	−6,386	− 1.4
8,559	16,669	7,310	3,479	2,354	5,320	+2,966	+126.0

CBeginning in 1972, data extracted from the Central Personnel Data File included records form employees with unspecified occupational series that are reported in the "Unspecified" occupational group. In 1980 this group includes approximately 3,000 employees who were reclassified by the General ACcounting Office to an occupation series that has not yet been established with OPM's Central Personnel Data File.

TABLE 1-5. Full-Time Civilian White-Collar Employment by Agency, Major Geographic Area, and Sex, October 31, 1980

Agency	ALL AREAS			WASHINGTON,	
	Total	Men	Women	Total	Men
Grand Total	1,985,057	1,217,940	767,117	280,871	150,615
General Accounting Office	5,131	3,433	1,698	3,146	1,930
Government Printing Office	2,402	1,157	1,245	2,097	1,002
Library of Congress	4,676	2,280	2,396	4,666	2,274
Other Legislative Branch	641	377	264	641	377
Judicial Branch	472	197	275	472	197
Exec Office of the President	1,446	684	762	1,443	683
Department of State	11,829	7,328	4,501	6,653	3,858
Department of the Treasury	111,633	55,213	56,420	15,948	8,889
Department of the Army	224,355	120,988	103,367	20,689	9,910
Department of the Navy	157,627	93,180	64,447	28,441	16,495
Department of the Air Force	131,840	71,139	60,701	4,378	1,821
Defense Logistics Agency	34,894	18,561	16,333	2,249	1,153
Other Defense Activities	27,130	15,174	11,956	9,511	5,907
Department of Justice	52,466	32,869	19,597	15,576	7,064
Department of Interior	59,674	39,451	20,223	7,912	4,783
Department of Agriculture	92,197	65,781	26,416	10,979	5,749
Department of Commerce	31,747	19,112	12,635	18,084	10,250
Department of Labor	22,183	12,532	9,651	7,605	3,532
Department of Health & Human Serv.	127,749	45,960	81,789	25,657	10,571
Department of Housing & Urban Development	16,018	8,142	7,876	4,360	1,995
Department of Transportation	64,380	51,965	12,415	9,295	5,897
Department of Energy	18,335	11,862	6,473	7,960	4,674
Department of Education	6,006	2,577	3,429	4,141	1,706
ACTION	1,543	701	842	800	329
Community Services Admin	1,041	516	525	392	189
Environmental Protection Agency	11,683	7,108	4,575	4,222	2,306
Equal Employment Opp Comm	3,226	1,389	1,837	753	302
Federal Communications Comm	2,038	1,103	935	1,493	797
Federal Deposit Insurance Corp	3,438	2,293	1,145	1,066	582
Federal Emergency Mgmt Agency	1,018	515	503	458	238
Federal Home Loan Bank Board	1,402	912	490	535	254
Federal Trade Commission	1,584	823	761	1,268	649
General Services Administration	21,311	11,705	9,606	8,320	4,804
Intl Communication Agency	3,831	2,341	1,490	2,776	1,555
Interstate Commerce Commission	1,870	1,058	812	1,331	710
Natl Aeronautics & Space Adm	21,801	16,756	5,045	4,777	3,355

D. C. SMSA	UNITED STATES EXCLUDING WASHINGTON, D. C. SMSA			OVERSEAS		
Women	Total	Men	Women	Total	Men	Women
130,256	1,659,156	1,044,310	614,846	45,030	23,015	22,015
1,216	1,912	1,448	464	73	55	18
1,095	305	155	150	–	–	–
2,392	–	–	–	10	6	4
264	–	–	–	–	–	–
275	–	–	–	–	–	–
760	–	–	–	3	1	2
2,795	1,099	610	589	4,077	2,960	1,117
7,059	94,837	45,700	49,137	848	624	224
10,779	189,648	105,269	84,379	14,018	5,809	8,209
11,946	125,645	74,691	50,954	3,541	1,994	1,547
2,557	123,471	67,755	55,716	3,991	1,563	2,428
1,096	32,472	17,293	15,179	173	115	58
3,604	9,148	6,476	2,762	8,471	2,791	5,680
8,512	36,114	25,279	10,835	776	526	250
3,129	51,555	34,494	17,061	207	174	33
5,230	80,337	59,328	21,009	881	704	177
7,834	13,477	8,687	4,790	186	175	11
4,073	14,512	8,951	5,561	66	49	17
15,086	101,339	35,041	66,298	753	348	405
2,365	11,497	6,052	5,445	161	95	66
3,398	54,496	45,540	8,956	589	528	61
3,286	10,369	7,182	3,187	6	6	–
2,435	1,865	871	994	–	–	–
471	587	259	328	156	113	43
203	649	327	322	–	–	–
1,916	7,450	4,794	2,656	11	8	3
451	2,473	1,087	1,386	–	–	–
696	538	301	237	7	5	2
484	2,347	1,687	640	45	24	21
220	552	272	280	8	5	3
281	867	658	209	–	–	–
619	316	174	142	–	–	–
3,516	12,948	6,872	6,076	43	29	14
1,221	228	168	60	827	618	208
621	539	348	191	–	–	–
1,422	17,003	13,380	3,623	21	21	–

(continued)

TABLE 1-5. (Continued)

Agency	ALL AREAS			WASHINGTON,	
	Total	Men	Women	Total	Men
Natl Labor Relations Board	2,610	1,311	1,299	819	363
Natl Science Foundation	1,176	566	610	1,173	563
Nuclear Regulatory Commission	3,020	2,095	925	2,312	1,546
Office of Personnel Management	6,428	2,720	3,708	3,196	1,382
Panama Canal Commission	1,143	805	338	2	–
Railroad Retirement Board	1,666	651	1,015	10	5
Securities & Exchange Commision	1,875	1,099	776	1,252	706
Small Business Administration	5,031	2,660	2,371	918	461
Smithsonian Institution	2,506	1,621	885	2,368	1,522
Tennessee Valley Authority	20,934	14,705	6,229	10	3
U.S. Intl Development Coop Agency	3,766	2,366	1,400	2,377	1,226
U.S. Postal Service	482,701	389,999	92,702	13,894	9,764
Veterans Administration	162,714	65,437	97,277	5,668	2,916
Other Executive Branch	8,870	4,723	4,147	6,778	3,371

D. C. SMSA	UNITED STATES EXCLUDING WASHINGTON, D. C. SMSA			OVERSEAS		
Women	Total	Men	Women	Total	Men	Women
456	1,770	935	835	21	13	8
610	2	2	–	1	1	–
766	708	549	159	–	–	–
1,814	3,219	1,333	1,886	13	5	8
2	21	9	12	1,120	796	324
5	1,656	646	1,010	–	–	–
546	623	393	230	–	–	–
457	4,108	2,195	1,913	5	4	1
946	95	72	23	43	27	16
7	20,920	14,698	6,222	4	4	–
1,151	28	22	6	1,361	1,118	243
4,130	467,940	379,451	88,489	867	784	83
2,752	155,437	61,642	93,795	1,609	879	730
3,407	2,054	1,314	740	38	38	–

Getting a
Civil Service Job

Applying for a federal civil service job can be likened to applying for a driver's license. Having decided you want to learn to drive, you take lessons, practice driving, and, when you feel you are ready, you take the test for a license. The test, presumably, measures your ability to handle the vehicle and to compete for space on the highway without incurring bodily harm to yourself, to others, or to the vehicle.

So it is with getting into government. Having set your sights on a federal career, your next step is to decide what kind of job you want, then preparing for it through education, training, and possibly some experience before taking the appropriate civil service examination.

However, unlike the driver's license, which you get immediately upon certification of your competence, the civil service system is a bit more complex. Assuming you meet all the requirements and get an eligible rating, you are placed on a list (called a "register") in the order of your score. But that's only the beginning.

Unless you are a veteran of a war in which the United States has been an active participant (World War II, Korea, Vietnam), your prospects for selection from the register are considerably reduced.

Under the Veterans' Preference Act of 1944, veterans with compensable disabilities are given ten points additional credit on their civil service examination rating and "float" to the top of the register, regardless of score, as long as they earn a passing grade. This entitlement extends to all but scientific and professional positions in grades GS-9 and higher. All other honorably discharged veterans routinely receive five points additional credit to a passing grade and take their place on the register in order of score. However, if you are a nonveteran and have the same score as a five-point "preference" veteran, the veteran must be given first choice for the vacancy. Because so few women are veterans, it has been a justifiable bone of contention among women that their chances for appointment are diminished. This is particularly true for professional and administrative positions. One is not likely to find a long list of veterans waiting for secretarial or clerical positions.

Before applying for a civil service examination, there are a few other decisions you must make: Where do you want to work? If your aim is a job in Washington, D.C., the hub of the bureaucracy, you should know that the cost of living in the metropolitan Washington area (which includes the suburbs of Maryland and Virginia) is among the highest in the nation. Rental properties are becoming ever scarcer. Taking advantage of the comparatively high income level of government employees, builders and developers and real estate owners are rapidly converting rental properties to condominiums and cooperatives and selling them at enormously overinflated prices. The same situation prevails in other large metropolitan areas (Los Angeles and San Francisco, for example). Investigate before you decide.

Is your heart set on working in a particular state or city? Then be sure the agency you are interested in has a field office in that locale.

Would you accept employment anywhere in the United States? Would you accept employment abroad? It is vital to explore the cost of living, especially abroad.

What is the lowest entrance salary you are prepared to accept? Before making that decision, you need to look over the kinds of jobs available in your chosen field, learn what is the entry level salary, and decide if you are willing and able to settle for what's being offered. Bear in mind that if you indicate a salary or grade level higher than what is being offered, you will not be considered for employment.

Would you be prepared to accept part-time employment? Short-term employment, that is, three months, six months, one year? The application for federal employment asks these questions.

Now that you have decided on your preferred geographic location, the salary you would accept, and the type of appointment (short-term, part-time, and so on), your next step is to look over the field to see the kinds of jobs for which the Office of Personnel Management is currently examining and, most important, the qualification requirements for eligibility.

On a quarterly basis the OPM publishes a one-page list called "Current Federal Civil Service Announcements." This sheet, as a general rule, is posted on the bulletin boards of all first-class post offices. It covers jobs throughout the United States, unless otherwise specified. Positions are listed under major headings, such as Administration, Finance and Accounting; Engineering; Physical Science and Mathematics; Social Science and Related Professions; Law Enforcement and Public Protection; Clerical; Health and Life Sciences.

For example, under the heading, Administration, Finance and Accounting, a typical announcement reads: "COMPUTER SPECIALIST: Programmer, Systems Analyst, Equipment Analyst, Specialist, GS-7 through GS-12. Some options and grade levels open in certain locations. See Announcement 420 and current amendment. Opportunities good to excellent, varying by locale and specialty. Good for GS-7 and 9 and excellent for GS-11 in Washington, D.C." A footnote indicates that jobs in foreign countries may also be filled from the list of qualified candidates.

The Washington, D.C. Area Office of OPM publishes a quarterly list called "Current Local Announcements for Positions in the Washington, D.C. Metropolitan Area." Using headings similar to those listed previously, the list provides examination announcement numbers, salary or grade, and status (whether the examination is open/closed or open for certain grade levels only), and a final column ranks opportunities for employment on a scale of one to four, with *one* being *excellent* and *four* being *poor*.

Finally, on a seasonal basis (Winter, Spring, Summer, Fall), OPM publishes a "Federal Employment Outlook," which summarizes "career fields and locales for which opportunities are most favorable for well-qualified applicants or for which chances for appointment are extremely limited." A disclaimer on this list states, "The description of a situation as favorable does not necessarily mean that there are specific vacancies at this time, but that we expect opportunities for the next one to three months to be very good. For more information about qualifications and application procedures, contact the nearest Federal Job Information Center. FJICs are usually listed in local telephone directories under "U.S. Government.' "

If you are not intrigued with the prospect of working in the nation's capital, but would prefer to stay in one of the states, visit the nearest OPM regional or area office for more specific information on available local opportunities.

Before getting your hopes too high, bear in mind that being among the best-qualified candidates is no assurance of getting a government job. The system is quite rigid with respect to the order of selection from a register.

For example. Let's assume Agency XYZ has a vacancy for a computer programmer. It provides OPM with a brief description of the job to be filled and requests a certificate (list) of eligibles. For each vacancy OPM provides approximately six names from the top of the register. The law requires agencies to select from among the top three candidates who indicate they are available. If among those candidates there are ten-point or five-point veterans willing to accept the position, your chances for selection, as indicated earlier, are greatly diminished.

Because of the barriers to selection resulting from the Veterans Preference Act, many professionally trained and educated women enter the government service through the secretarial or clerical ranks in hopes of "getting a foot in the door." Sometimes it works. More often it does not. The author discourages women with college degrees in specialized fields from taking secretarial or clerical jobs. After all, what man doesn't want a college-educated secretary? Once he has her, he is not about to let her go. I have run across far too many cases in my long career and have counseled many frustrated, overqualified women who were "locked in" to positions far beneath their level of competence. I cited one such case in the Introduction. There are thousands more.

On the other hand, and this may seem like a contradiction, with the momentum of the women's movement, which has contributed to the enactment of legislation mandating equal employment opportunities for women and minorities, a special program now exists in federal government called "The Federal Women's Program," which requires agencies to develop programs to provide for employment and advancement opportunities for women. All major departments and agencies have appointed federal women's program managers whose primary function is to assist management in developing programs to provide upward mobility opportunities for women at all levels through established affirmative action plans.

Women themselves have become more aware of their legal rights to equal opportunity in the marketplace. In droves they have been flocking to courses on assertive behavior, self-awareness, career development, women in management, and the like. Thus reinforced, these women are becoming more courageous in demanding a chance to demonstrate their potential and ultimately reach their goals. Some are succeeding.

This is not to suggest that sex discrimination has been erased. Far from it. But there are significant signs of progress that warrant a smattering of optimism for the future. Among the signs is the not-so-subtle pressure on managers to comply with affirmative action policies.

Case in point. The OPM issued a "Manager's Handbook" in 1980 that emphasizes what managers must know and do about dealing with their employees. One chapter deals exclusively with the manager's responsibility for ensuring equal employment opportunity for all employees under his or her jurisdiction. It proclaims, "If you are a GS-13 or above supervisor or management official, your organizational performance will determine your merit pay increases. Most agencies are giving more emphasis to the Equal Employment Opportunity efforts of their managers in evaluating their performance. Your agency will be taking a close look at your unit's EEO profile and at the actions you take to meet your EEO responsibilities."

By using this pocketbook approach, it was thought managers would bury their prejudices and apply equal justice to all employees regardless of race, color, sex, or national origin.

On the subject of affirmative action to implement the EEO program, the Manager's Handbook states: "Affirmative employment efforts include identifying possible barriers to the employment and advancement of identified groups, and working to eliminate such barriers. They also include creative efforts to modify the existing system to assure that minorities, women and the handicapped have equal access to employment and training opportunities."

These caveats to managers are all well and good. But human nature being what it is, managers have not been rushing to seek out women to promote or train for higher-level jobs. It remains, therefore, for each individual, so motivated, to take the initiative to plan ahead and design a personal career path.

Now to the mechanics of applying for a civil service job. Having decided what you want to do and where you want to work, check with the Federal Job Information Center (FJIC) nearest you to ascertain if there is an open examination announcement for positions in your field. Obtain a copy of the examination announcement, study the qualification requirements carefully. If you find you meet the criteria, your next step is to obtain a handful of employment applications, Standard Form 171 (SF 171), Personal Qualifications Statement. These forms, properly executed, are the key that unlocks job opportunities for you. If the key is not properly cut, it won't fit the lock. So it is with your SF-171. If it is not sharp and crisp and finely honed, it may keep you from getting a rating and a place on the register.

There is neither magic nor mystery to completing the SF-171. As its title indicates, it is a "personal qualifications statement." A statement of your experience, education, and training that you believe make you the best qualified person for the job. Now your task is to prove it.

Before you put pen to paper, examine carefully the specific knowledge and skills required for the particular job. Thoroughly assess your own skills and the skills the organization is seeking. Recency of experience is heavily weighted in judging your eligibility. You would be wasting your time and energy by applying for a job in any occupation without appropriate and relevant credentials.

You are probably thinking, "Anybody knows that!"

Let me assure you, not everyone is as wise as you. I have seen applications for accountant positions, for example, from individuals who had had a year or two of high school bookkeeping some ten years earlier, but no actual "accounting" courses nor recent experience in the field. It's naive to assume such applications would even be considered.

By the same token, nine semester hours of college credit in psychology does not a psychologist make, nor would a couple of courses in physics qualify one for an engineering position.

So it is important to study the examination announcement carefully to learn what specific education, training, and experience are required before applying. If you do not meet the minimum requirements, don't bother to apply. However, by analyzing the requirements, you can learn what additional training or education you might need in order to become eligible at some future date. You might want to go back to school for a few additional specialized courses. In the long run, such effort could pay dividends.

Volunteer work is creditable toward your total experience, depending upon the amount of time devoted to the particular activity. For example, if you served as treasurer of a club, sorority, church group, or a professional organization for a year or more, be sure to include it, especially if you are applying for a position in the field of accounting. (Volunteer work is discussed in greater depth in Chapter 3.)

But remember—whatever you claim as experience—paid or volunteer—must be verifiable. So be truthful.

After you have carefully reviewed the examination announcement and have determined that you meet the qualification requirements, start to prepare a rough draft of your SF-171. This will no doubt be the beginning of many drafts before you are satisfied with the final product. And that's as it should be.

At this point you become a salesperson and the product you are selling is YOU. How you market yourself can make the difference between getting or not getting on a register and ultimately being employed.

The application should be prepared in such fashion as to stimulate the interest of the personnel technician who will review it. More than two million applications come in to OPM annually! Your application should be neatly typed, well spaced, and unencumbered by a bundle of attachments attesting to your credentials. First impressions of an application are as important as first impressions of you personally. Remember, not only will your application be used to rate you on the examination; it will also be reviewed by an operating official in the agency to which it may be referred to fill a vacancy.

It is not unusual for interviewers to sift through stacks of applications and pull the ones that look worthy of consideration—not those that are handwritten, or loaded down with sheafs of documents, such as descriptions of former positions, letters of reference, or samples of work.

This is not to suggest that one never submits attachments. But discretion and judgment must be exercised. For example, if you are applying for a job as a public information specialist (writer) or graphic artist, the announcement may ask for samples of your work to accompany the application. If such is the case, submit no more than one or two (depending upon the length) and indicate that more will be presented at the time of your interview. If you get an eligible rating and are referred for an interview, be sure to bring additional samples of your creative work. But do not bring a Master's or PhD thesis—no one will read it.

Avoid the use of "canned" job descriptions in recounting your past experience. There is little room, as you will see, on the SF-171 for extensive descriptions of your experience. Not that you are confined to the eight lines provided on the form, but if you cannot describe what you have done in a few well-chosen sentences and in your own words, chances are you will not be considered.

Personnel specialists can spot in a minute the stilted, formal language used on company-prepared job descriptions (especially from federal agencies) and are likely to toss your application in the "to-be-looked-at-later-if-time-permits-and-no-better-applicant-is-available pile." More often than not, there are better applicants and the "pile" never gets reviewed.

For professional positions, beginning at the GS-9 level, no written examinations are required. Eligibility is determined on the basis of education and experience, including volunteer work. That's why careful preparation of your application is so important. (See "Hints for Preparing a SF-171" on page 73.)

Brevity is important. If you are more at ease using personal pronouns, do so. But concentrate on active verbs that accurately and succinctly describe what you have done as it relates to the position for which you are applying. For example, *wrote, edited, processed, analyzed, researched, developed, reviewed,* and so on. Be sure to write about what *you* have done, not what the office or your boss was responsible for.

Type your duties statements on plain bond paper, taking as much space as you need, within reason, then cut and paste the form so that all the information, job by job, will appear, in reverse chronological order, with present or most recent job heading the list. If you prefer to use ruled lines, cut and paste blank, lined spaces from extra copies of the SF-171. Prospective employers will be more inclined to read your application in its entirety if they do not have to flip back and forth searching for continuation sheets, addenda, attachments, and other extraneous material. (See samples of expanded experience blocks at the end of this chapter.)

Your application must be relevant to the specific job for which you are applying. If the job requires a major emphasis, for example, on mathematics skills and knowledge, and you have them, emphasize how and where you acquired the skills or used them on a previous job. If you were an outstanding mathematics student, brag a little—especially if you have had no previous employment experience.

If you have been employed by the same company or agency for a long period of time and have received one or more promotions, use a separate block on the SF-171 to describe what you did in each job, which led to the promotion(s). Under "reason for leaving," indicate it was for promotion.

Until August 1982 the vehicle for entry into professional and administrative careers was the PACE examination (Professional and Administrative Career Examination). However, as the result of a civil suit (Luevano v. Devine), alleging that the examination discriminated against blacks and Hispanics, the United States District Court for the District of Columbia decreed the examination be discontinued to eliminate further adverse impact on the appointment of blacks and Hispanics to positions formerly covered by PACE.

Subsequently all existing PACE registers of eligibles were cancelled and a different, more complex procedure for external appointments was adopted. How long these new hiring procedures will remain in effect is anyone's guess.

In the absence of lists of qualified applicants being maintained by the Office of Personnel Management for the majority of occupations covered by PACE, interested individuals should apply directly to the agency in which they wish to work.

Periodically the College Relations Office of OPM in Washington, D.C. issues a publication called "By the Way." It is distributed to college placement officers and contains useful information about employment prospects for the college student. If you are in college at present, ask your placement office to show you a copy.

Two other publications should be of interest to the college student: "First See US," is designed for potential applicants seeking information about how federal jobs are filled, how to apply, and requirements for employment. The second one is called "Working for the USA," and provides more detailed coverage of subjects found in "First See US." Single copies are available, free of charge, through OPM regional and area offices.

If you are a college student, especially an undergraduate, aspiring to a career in public service—or in the private sector, for that matter—it is important to know something about anticipated employment needs for the time when you will be ready to enter the job market.

An excellent source of such information is "The Job Outlook for College Graduates Through 1990," published by the Bureau of Labor Statistics. Copies ought to be available in college libraries and placement offices. They may also be purchased from the Superintendent of Documents, U.S. Government Printing Office, Washington, D.C.

Annually the Bureau of Labor Statistics publishes the "Occupational Outlook Handbook," a rather massive document which, as stated in its Prefatory Note, ". . . contains information on job duties, educational requirements, employment outlook, and earnings for several hundred occupations and 35 industries. The Handbook information is based on data received from a variety of sources, including business firms, trade associations, labor unions, professional societies, educational institutions, and government agencies, and represents the most current and comprehensive information available."

It is an established fact that nine out of ten women will be in the labor force for a major portion of their adult lives. It would be wise to prepare in advance for a career in a field where job opportunities exist. The "Handbook" is a good place to start your research.

If public service is your goal and you are a college undergraduate, it would be to your advantage to get a summer job in a federal agency where you can see for yourself what kind of work is being done, what kinds of skills are valued above others, what prospects there may be for full-time employment when you graduate, and how the bureaucracy functions. Summer jobs in government are none too plentiful and it is of utmost importance that you apply early—by January or February, as soon as OPM announces it is accepting applications for summer employment. Better still, go directly to the agency of your choice and inquire about such jobs.

If you are an undergraduate and cannot qualify for a professional position, you may want to consider taking a job as a clerk or typist for a couple of months. It is a great opportunity to explore whether government is indeed the place for you.

Many young women have taken summer jobs in government between freshman and sophomore years and demonstrated their potential for higher-level positions. So competent were they that they were invited back each summer and after graduation were offered full-time positions. Since so many agencies have direct hiring authority, this can be one of the best avenues to a government career.

Regrettably, some recent presidents of the United States and other politicians have been guilty of maligning the federal employee because they think that's what the folks back home want to hear. They would like you to believe that government employees sit around all day drinking coffee and discussing the latest football or baseball scores.

I can assure you, some of the most dedicated and knowledgeable people in the nation are on federal payrolls working for the betterment of humankind in every discipline. For example, if the Department of Agriculture did not require inspection and grading of meat and meat byproducts, you might be buying dog, cat, and horseflesh at your supermarket counters.

Let's not forget the work of a woman doctor at the National Institutes of Health who exposed the hazards of Thalidomide, which caused the birth of babies without limbs.

These are but two glaring examples of the work of government employees. Thousands more could be cited.

The demand for certain specialized skills is increasing. In fact, between 1960 and 1980, the number of engineers in federal service increased by more than 50 percent, to 98,931; the number of computer specialists increased by 600 percent to 46,361; the number of attorneys nearly doubled to 15,530; and the number of social scientists, psychologists, and welfare workers increased by more than 230 percent to 58,166.

Knowing where the opportunities exist, women should be preparing to enter these fields.

Though the majority (70 percent) of women are in the lower-paying jobs, there is increasing evidence of gradual advancement to higher-level positions. Women have to work toward such goals harder than men.

A word of caution. It could take from six months to a year from the time you qualify on a civil service examination until you may be invited for an interview or asked if you are still available for employment. One reason is the severe reduction in the federal workforce proposed by the Reagan Administration.

While layoffs and furloughs are taking place in many agencies, others are hiring. Retirements, deaths, and resignations will create other vacancies. So don't become completely discouraged.

By the same token, if you can avoid it, don't lower your self-esteem by accepting a government job that knowingly underutilizes your skills and training and holds little or no promise for advancement.

Stay in touch with the department or agency where you want to work. A periodic telephone call or, better still, a personal visit will help keep your name and face before the hiring official. Be persistent, but graciously so. Your task is to convince the agency it needs and wants you. It is the toughest selling job you will ever do in your life. But the rewards may well be worth the effort.

The following material on "How to Get a Job in the Federal Government," was prepared by the Inter-Agency Minority and Female Recruiters Association and is reprinted with their permission.

Getting a Government Job

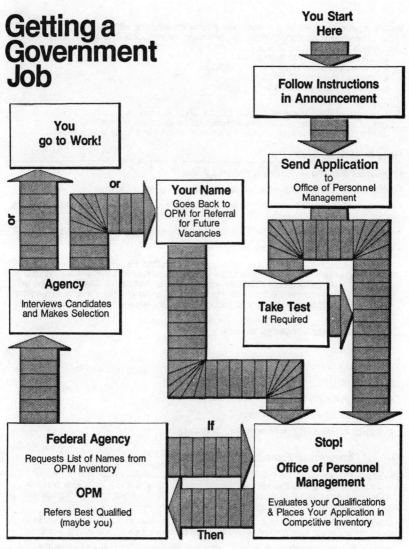

You Start Here

Follow Instructions in Announcement

Send Application
to
Office of Personnel Management

Take Test
If Required

You go to Work!

or

Your Name
Goes Back to OPM for Referral for Future Vacancies

Agency
Interviews Candidates and Makes Selection

or

Federal Agency
Requests List of Names from OPM Inventory

OPM
Refers Best Qualified (maybe you)

If

Then

Stop!

Office of Personnel Management
Evaluates your Qualifications & Places Your Application in Competitive Inventory

---

Where and How to Obtain Information

A. The Office of Personnel Management (formerly the U.S. Civil Service Commission) maintains **Federal Job Information Centers** across the country to provide local job information. Look under "U.S. Government" in the white pages of the metropolitan area phone directories for the center nearest you. If none is listed in your directory, dial 800-555-1212 for the toll free number of a Federal Job Information Center in your state.

B. **Call or write the center in your state. You provide the following information:**
1. The level of education you have completed and the amount of paid and unpaid experience you have;
2. The kind of work that interests you;
3. The area or areas where you want to work;
4. The lowest salary you will accept;
5. Whether you are a veteran.

C. **Request**
1. A copy of examination announcements for which you qualify;
2. Copies of blank application forms needed for the exam you will apply for;
3. Provide a clearly written name and address to which these forms should be sent.

Hints on How to Apply

- Remember that jobs are located in Federal agencies.
- Job announcements are found in personnel offices at individual agencies.
- Check your telephone directory white pages under the heading "United States Government" to locate nearby Federal agencies.
- Call the number listed and ask for the address and phone number of the personnel offices.
- Visit personnel offices and ask for listing of vacancies.
- Submit application forms for jobs in which you are interested. Be sure to follow all procedures in the examination (job) announcement. The Office of Personnel Management will evaluate your application and issue a Notice of Results which may be a "Notice of Rating" telling you the grade level(s) and occupations for which you have qualified for or a letter acknowledging the receipt of your application. A Notice of Rating or letter of acknowledgement is not an offer of a Federal job.

Sources to Locate Vacancies Include:

1) Newspapers

2) Employees of the Agency

3) Agency officials

4) Special publications

5) IMFRA Career Assistance Center

6) College or university placement offices or professors

General Categories of Federal Jobs

Professional Occupations are those requiring knowledge in a field of science or learning characteristically acquired through education or training equivalent to a bachelor's or higher degree with major study in or pertinent to the specialized field, as distinguished from general education, i.e., engineer, accountant, biologist, chemist.

Administrative Occupations are those which are typically gained through progressive responsible experience or college level general education, i.e., personnel specialist, administrative officer.

Technical Occupations are those involving work typically associated with, and supportive of a professional or administrative field, which is non-routine in nature, i.e., computer technician, electronic technician.

Clerical Occupations are those involving structured work in support of office, business, or fiscal operations, i.e., clerk-typist, mail and file clerk.

Other Occupations are those that cannot be related to the above, i.e., painters, carpenters, and laborers.

How to Fill Out Federal Application Forms

A. Upon receipt of SF-171 or other Federal application forms and job announcement, do the following:

1) Read job announcement thoroughly to familiarize yourself with the specific requirements listed in job announcement which interest you.

2) Begin the process of completing the SF-171 by remembering the following general guidelines:

   a. Always use a typewriter. If this is not possible, write neatly and clearly in ink.

   b. Make a master copy and do not sign and date. Photo copy additional copies and sign and date each copy when necessary for distribution.

   c. Before you prepare your SF-171, review your life experiences, especially those which can enhance the position for which you are applying. Make a list of specific activities, duties, knowledges, and work experience.

3) **Begin with page 1 of the SF-171.**

Standard Form 171

Personal Qualifications Statement

IMPORTANT
READ THE FOLLOWING INSTRUCTIONS CAREFULLY BEFORE FILLING OUT YOUR STATEMENT

● You must furnish all requested information. The information you provide will be used to determine your qualifications for employment. DO NOT SEND A RESUME IN LIEU OF COMPLETING THIS STATEMENT.

● If you fail to answer all questions on your Statement fully and accurately, you may delay consideration of your Statement and may lose employment opportunities. See the Privacy Act Information on the reverse of this sheet.

● So that it is understood that you did not omit an item, please write the letters "N/A" (Not Applicable) beside those items that do not apply to you, unless instructions indicate otherwise.

Personal Qualifications Statement
Read Instructions before completing form

Form Approved:
OMB No. 50-R0387

1. Kind of position *(job)* you are filing for *(or title and number of announcement)*

2. Options for which you wish to be considered *(if listed in the announcement)*

3. Home phone		4. Work phone		
Area Code	Number	Area Code	Number	Extension

5. Sex *(for statistics only)*   Male   Female

6. Other last names ever used

Name *(Last, First, Middle)*

Street address or RFD no. *(include apartment no., if any)*

City	State	ZIP Code

8. Birthplace *(City & State, or foreign country)*

9. Birth date *(Month, day, year)*   10. Social Security Number

DO NOT WRITE IN THIS BLOCK
FOR USE OF EXAMINING OFFICE ONLY

Material   Submitted   Returned

Entered register:

Notations:

Form reviewed:
Form approved:

Option	Grade	Earned Rating	Preference	Aug. Rating
			☐ 5 Points (Tent)	
			☐ 10 Pts 30% or More Comp Dis	
			☐ 10 Pts Less Than 30% Comp Dis	

ANNOUNCEMENT NO.

STATEMENT

Page 1 of the SF-171

1. Position
Fill in the position category or name and announcement number supplied on job announcement.

2. Options
Fill in "Any job for which qualified."

3, 4. Home and Work Phones
Your home phone and work phone numbers.

5. Preferred Title
Pick the one you want.

6. Other Last Names
This item is especially important for women who may have been married or remarried. Be sure to indicate maiden name and previous married name.

7, 8, 9, 10. Name, Address, Birthplace, Birthdate, and Social Security Number
Fill in every block completely. If your address changes after you have applied for an evaluation at OPM, be sure to inform OPM by letter.

11. Previous Federal Employment
Indicate where, when, and how long.

12. Current Application on File with OPM
This is important. If this is your first time filling out a SF-171, you are obviously not on file with OPM.

13. Pay or Grade
Fill in your desired salary.

14. Availability
Put whatever date you expect to be available.

15. Temporary Employment
Willingness to accept a temporary assignment can be a good way of getting in the door. If this is offered, weigh the advantages and disadvantages as they apply to your situation.

16. Other Employment
State kinds and titles.

17. Where You Will Accept a Job
State location.

18. Travel
Check what is feasible for you and your circumstances.

19. Part-Time Positions
Willingness to accept a part-time position can be a good way of getting in the door.

20. Veteran Preference
State whether or not you are a veteran. You may gain some added advantage by having 5 to 10 points added to numerical rating or an OPM exam.

Page 2 of the SF-171

21. Experience
Be complete.

The first question in this rather lengthy section on experience concerns whether or not personnel staff may contact your present employer. A "no" answer here will not affect your employment opportunities, but if you do answer "no," try to provide some form of evaluation, such as a performance evaluation or letter of recommendation.

    a. Use the word "I" instead of "the incumbent" or "he/she." Use "I" sparingly by indicating your responsibilities, i.e., "Was directly responsible for..."

b. Use "active" verbs—a verb with a direct object is an active verb. Example: I typed letters.

c. Be complete. Use all the lines allotted to each job and write more if you need to on plain white paper. Be sure to number the attachments with the item number, your birthdate, and name.

d. Include all major duties of each job.

e. Use your own words—not words from position descriptions.

f. Be specific about what tasks you performed; do not summarize; explain fully.

g. Include volunteer work.

h. Note that the form asks you to list your present job first and then the one you had before that one, and so on. Experience acquired more than 15 years ago may be summarized in one block if it is not applicable to the type of position applying for.

i. Write a draft of your experience first. Then rewrite your draft as many times as is necessary to produce a complete, well-written description of duties.

j. Don't abbreviate. Don't use acronyms unless you explain the meaning in the first use.

k. Include brief excerpts from official or unofficial letters in which your work was praised. Mention job-related awards.

l. Don't type your material into one long, unending paragraph, especially if you choose to use more space than that provided on the form. Break up your description into short sentences or paragraphs. Use headings. Aim for a clear, well-organized presentation to ensure that it will be read by the personnel specialist.

Page 3 of the SF-171

22. Special Qualifications and Skills

Include membership in professional organizations, title of any informational material written even if unpublished. Indicate examples of public speaking including Sunday School work, etc.; list hobbies relevant to positions for which you are applying; indicate typing skill.

23. Education

Be sure to show all the training you have had. Include the names of schools, location, dates attended, subject studied, number of classroom or credit hours received, and any other pertinent data. (Credit hours refer to the number of units, whether quarter or semester, you earned for a college course.) As in other items, you may have to add separate sheets to be complete. You may also want to include a college transcript.

23-G. Other Schools and Training

Include in-service workshops, seminars, professional conferences, private study, correspondence courses, military training, leadership orientation, career specialty training, and others. Be sure to give all the details requested, including time involved, so that it may be properly rated. Do not neglect the area of personal development and study.

24. Honors, Awards, and Fellowships

Many people are modest about awards. Honors and awards don't have to be earth-shaking to be included. Cite scholarships, letters of commendation from your supervisor, safety awards, suggestion awards (you might describe the suggestion and its benefits briefly), community awards and nominations, and election to honorary societies or groups. Your most recent awards are usually the most relevant. However, if you received only a few awards list them all even though all were presented some years ago.

25. Foreign Language

Any familiarity with a foreign language should be mentioned. Be honest in evaluating your abilities.

26. References

Use people who know you.

Use people who know your work.

Use people who can be reached and include their phone numbers.

Don't list people who are out of the country, have no phone, or whose whereabouts are unknown to you.

Ask your references for permission to use their names.

Page 4 of the SF-171

27-34. These questions are important. Read them carefully and answer yes or no as directed for each one. U.S.citizenship is required for most permanent civil service positions.

35. This space may be used to continue answers from any other question.

Your Signature

a. Read the closing information carefully.

b. Make photo copies.

Do not sign the original SF-171. Sign and date each copy as you submit it for a specific vacancy.

Part-Time Positions and Summer Jobs

I. Part-Time Positions

Part-time positions—16 to 32 hours per week—are available in agencies throughout the Federal Government. Applications should be made directly to the personnel office in the agency of your choice.

II. Summer Jobs

Summer employment opportunities for high school, college, medical and dental students are available but limited throughout the Federal Government. Contact your Federal Job Information Center in October or November for summer job announcements.

a. Information Applicable to All Summer Jobs

Summer jobs are located in Federal agencies and departments throughout the United States. The majority of jobs are in large metropolitan areas. If you wish information on employment opportunities in an agency, you should contact the agency directly to find out if applications are being accepted for summer employment. Agency addresses may be obtained from Federal Job Information Centers or from the white pages of local telephone directories under the listing "United States Government."

b. Members of Family

You may not be considered for a summer job in the same department or agency in which your father or mother is employed unless you are selected for a job from an agency list of eligibles established in accordance with special procedures. Check with the agency regarding their procedures.

c. Who May Apply

If you meet the minimum qualification requirements for the job to be filled, age and citizenship requirements, and general standards for Federal employment, your name will be entered on the list of eligibles in the agency where you apply.

III. Special Placement Assistance for the Physically Handicapped

Persons who have severe physical handicaps which may limit their activity in performing a job may qualify for special placement assistance from the Office of Personnel Management. For more information, contact a Federal Job Information Center. Handicapped applicants may also contact Federal agencies in which they would like to work.

IV. Postal Service Jobs

Questions about Postal Service employment should be directed to the Post Office where employment is desired.

V. Jobs in Alaska, Guam, Hawaii, Puerto Rico, and the Virgin Islands

Because of the limited number of jobs in Alaska, Guam, Hawaii, Puerto Rico, and the Virgin Islands, residents of these areas will receive first consideration for employment. Other candidates will be considered only when there are no qualified residents available.

Working Conditions, Benefits, and Holidays

1. Hours of Work

The usual government workweek is 40 hours. Most government employees work 8 hours, 5 days a week, Monday through Friday, but, in some cases, the nature of the work may call for a different workweek. As in any other business, employees sometimes have to work overtime. If you are required to work overtime, you will either be paid for overtime or given time off to make up for the extra time you worked.

2. Advancement

Most agencies fill vacancies, whenever possible, by promoting their own employees.

Federal employees receive on-the-job training. They may also participate in individualized career development programs and receive job-related training in their own agency, in other agencies, or outside the government (for example, in industrial plants and universities). It is not always necessary to move to a new job in order to advance in grade. Sometimes an employee's work assignments change a great deal in the ordinary course of business. The job "grows." When that happens, it is time for a position classifier to study the job again. If he/she finds that the job should be put in a higher grade because of increased difficulty or responsibility of the duties, the change is made.

3. Efficiency Counts

At intervals, employees are rated on their job performance. In most agencies, the ratings are "outstanding," "satisfactory," and "unsatisfactory."

Employees with "outstanding" ratings receive extra credit for retention in layoffs. An employee whose rating is "unsatisfactory" may be dismissed or assigned to another position with duties which he/she can be expected to learn to do satisfactorily.

4. Incentive Awards

Government agencies encourage their employees to suggest better or simpler ways, or more economical ways, of doing their jobs. They may give a cash award to an employee for a suggestion or invention that results in money savings or improved service. They may also reward outstanding job performance or other acts that are deserving of recognition.

5. Vacation and Sick Leave

Most Federal employees earn annual leave for vacation and other purposes, according to the number of years (civilian plus creditable military service) they have been in the Federal service. They earn it at the rate of 13 days a year for the first 3 years of service and 20 days a year for the next 12 years of service. After 15 years, they earn 26 days of annual leave each year.

Sick leave is earned at the rate of 13 days a year. You can use this leave for illnesses serious enough to keep you away from your work and for appointments with a doctor, dentist, or optician. Sick leave that is not used can be saved for future use.

6. Injury Compensation

The government provides liberal compensation benefits, including medical care, for employees who suffer injuries in the performance of official duty. Death benefits are also provided if an employee dies as a result of such injuries.

7. Group Life Insurance

As a Federal employee, you may have low-cost term life insurance without taking a physical examination. Two kinds of insurance are provided: (1) life insurance, and (2) accidental death and dismemberment insurance.

8. Health Benefits

The government sponsors a voluntary health insurance program for Federal employees. The program offers a variety of plans to meet individual needs, including basic coverage and major medical protection against costly illnesses. The government contributes part of the cost of premiums and the employee pays the balance through payroll deductions.

9. Retirement

Seven percent of a career or career-conditional employee's salary goes into a retirement fund. This seven percent comes out of every paycheck. This money is withheld as the employee's share of the cost of providing him or her or his/her survivors with an income after he/she has completed his/her working career.

If you leave the government before you complete five years of service, the money you put into the retirement fund can be returned to you. If you leave after completing five years of service, you have a choice of having your money returned or leaving it in the fund. If you leave it in the fund, you will get an annuity starting when you are age 62.

10. Holidays

Government workers are entitled to the following nine regular holidays each year:

New Year's Day, January 1

Washington's Birthday, 3rd Monday in February

Memorial Day, Last Monday in May

Independence Day, July 4

Labor Day, 1st Monday in September

Columbus Day, 2nd Monday in October

Veterans Day, November 11

Thanksgiving Day, 4th Thursday in November

Christmas Day, December 25

When Inauguration Day falls on a regularly scheduled workday, employees in the Washington metropolitan area get a tenth holiday.

Glossary of Selected Federal Personnel Terms

Affirmative Action — A policy that requires Federal agencies to take positive steps to insure equal opportunity in employment, development, advancement, and treatment of all employees and applications for employment regardless of race, color, sex, religion, age, national origin, or physical or mental handicap. Affirmative Action also requires that specific actions be directed at the special problems and unique concerns in assuring equal employment opportunity for minorities, and women.

Agency — Any department or independent establishment of the Federal Government, including a Government-owned or controlled corporation.

Application Forms — Documents, usually the Standard Form 171 and supplementary forms, completed by persons seeking Federal employment. The forms require information about the applicant's qualifications for the positions for which he/she is applying and about his/her suitability for Federal service.

Appointment — The process of selecting a person and assigning him/her to a position.

Appointment, Career-Conditional — The tenure of a permanent employee who has not yet completed 3 years of creditable, substantially continuous Federal service.

Appointment, Competitive — Employment of a person after competition with others for the same position. Includes appointments from the register, some appointments from the applicant supply file, and most appointments under the Merit Promotion Program.

Appointment, Noncompetitive — Employment without competing with others, in the sense that it is done without regard to OPM registers or the priorities of applicant supply files. Includes reinstatements, transfers, reassignments, demotions, and some promotions.

Career — Tenure of a permanent employee in the competitive service who has completed three years of substantially continuous creditable Federal service.

Certificate — A list of eligibles ranked, according to regulations, for appointment or promotion consideration. A more useful term is "candidate list."

Competitive Service — Federal positions normally filled through open competitive examination (hence the term "competitive service") under civil service rules and regulations. About 62 percent of all Federal positions are in the competitive service.

Eligible — Any applicant for appointment or promotion who meets the minimum qualification requirements.

Entrance Level Position — A position in an occupation at the beginning level grade.

Examination — A means of measuring, in a practical and suitable manner, qualifications of applicants for employment in specific positions.

Federal Personnel Manual (FPM) — The official publication containing Federal personnel regulations and guidance. Also contains the code of Federal civil service law, selected Executive orders pertaining to Federal employment, and civil service rules.

General Schedule (GS) — The graded pay system as presented by Chapter 51 of Title 5, United States Code, for classifying positions.

Grade — All classes of positions which, although different with respect to kind or subject matter of work, are sufficiently equivalent as to (1) level of difficulty and responsibility, and (2) level of qualification requirements of the work to warrant the inclusion of such classes of positions within one range of rates of basic compensation.

Job Title — The formal name of a position as determined by official classification standards.

Journeyman Level — (Full Performance Level) — The lowest level of a career ladder position at which an employee has learned the full range of duties in a specific occupation. All jobs below full performance level are developmental levels, through which each employee in the occupation may progress to full performance.

Leave, Annual — Time allowed to employees for vacation and other absences for personal reasons.

Merit Promotion Program — The system under which agencies consider an employee for internal personnel actions on the basis of personal merit.

Personnel Action — The process necessary to appoint, separate, reinstate, or make other changes affecting an employee (e.g., change in position, assignment, tenure, etc.)

Position — A specific job consisting of all the current major duties and responsibilities assigned or delegated by management.

Position Classification — Analyzing and categorizing jobs by occupational group, series, class, and grade according to like duties, responsibilities, and qualification requirements.

Position Description — An official written statement of the major duties, responsibilities, and supervisory relationships of a position.

Preference, Compensable Disability ("CP") — Ten-point preference awarded to a veteran separated under honorable conditions from active duty, who receives compensation of 10 percent or more for a service connected disability. Eligible "CP" veterans are placed at the top of civil service lists of eligibles for positions at GS-9 or higher.

Preference, 30 Percent or More, Disability ("CPS") — A disabled veteran whose disability is rated at 30 percent or more, entitled to special preference in appointment and during reduction in force.

Preference, Disability ("XP") — Ten-point preference in hiring for a veteran separated under honorable conditions from active duty and who has a service-connected disability or receives compensation, pension, or disability retirement from the VA or a uniformed service.

Preference, Mother ("XP") — Ten-point preference to which the mother of a deceased or disabled military veteran may be entitled.

Preference, Spouse ("XP") — Ten-point preference to which a disabled military veteran's spouse may be entitled.

Preference, Tentative ("TP") — Five-point veteran preference tentatively awarded an eligible who served on active duty during specified periods and was separated from military service under honorable conditions. It must be verified by the appointing officer.

Preference, Veteran — The statutory right to special advantage in appointment or separations; based on a person's discharge under honorable conditions from the armed forces, for a service-connected disability. Not applicable to the Senior Executive Service.

Preference, Widow or Widower ("XP") — Ten-point preference to which a military veteran's widow or widower may be entitled.

Probationary Period — A trial period which is a condition of the initial competitive appointment. Provides the final indispensable test of ability, that of actual performance on the job.

Promotion — A change of an employee to a higher grade when both the old and new positions are under the same job classification system and pay schedule, or to a position with higher pay in a different job classification system and pay schedule.

Promotion, Career — Promotion of an employee without current competition when: (1) he/she had earlier been competitively selected from a register or under competitive promotion procedures for an assignment intended as a matter of record to be preparation for the position being filled; or (2) the position is reconstituted at a higher grade because of additional duties and responsibilities.

Promotion, Competitive — Selection of a current or former Federal civil service employee for a higher grade position, using procedures that compare the candidates on merit.

Qualification Review Board (QRB) — A panel normally used to evaluate and group candidates for positions to be filled under the Merit Promotion Program.

Register — A list of eligible applicants compiled in the order of their relative standing for referral to Federal jobs, after competitive civil service examination.

Senior Executive Service — A separate personnel system for persons who set policy and administer programs at the top levels of the Government (equivalent to GS-16 through Executive Level IV).

Standard Form 171 (Personal Qualifications Statement) — Used in applying for a Federal position through a competitive examination.

Listing of Federal Job Information Centers

Source:
United States Office of Personnel Management

The Office of Personnel Management operates Federal Job Information Centers (FJICs) in the cities listed below. FJICs can provide general information on Federal employment, explain how to apply for specific jobs, and supply application materials.

You can get information by mail, by telephone, or by visiting an FJIC. The easiest method, if you want information or application materials for a specific job or occupation and can identify it clearly, usually is to write. All FJICs operate Monday through Friday (except holidays), but the number of hours each one is open to the public varies from one FJIC to another. Many do not handle walk-in traffic or telephone inquiries for more than four or six hours a day. Because of the large number of people who seek information by telephone, the lines are frequently busy or callers must hold for a time before an information specialist can speak with them. To alleviate this problem, some FJICs provide recorded telephone messages. These messages give the hours of service for the FJIC, and sometimes provide general job information as well.

OPM provides Federal employment information to State Job Service (State Employment Security) offices and, for college-entry jobs, to college placement offices. In addition, many Federal agencies recruit directly for their own vacancies and provide a variety of information services.

Federal Job Information Centers that also provide information about jobs with city, county, or State governments are identified below with a (•).

Federal Job Information Centers

Alabama
Huntsville:
Southerland Building
806 Governors Dr., N.W., 35801
(205) 453-5070

Alaska
Anchorage:
Federal Bldg. & U.S. Courthouse
701 C St., P.O. Box 22, 99513
(907) 271-5821

Arizona
Phoenix:
522 N. Central Ave., 85004
(602) 261-4736

Arkansas
Little Rock:
Federal Bldg., Rm. 1319
700 W. Capitol Ave., 72201
(501) 378-5842

California
Los Angeles:
Linder Bldg.
845 S. Figueroa, 90017
(213) 688-3360

Sacramento:
Federal Bldg., 650 Capitol Mall, 95814
(916) 440-3441

San Diego:
880 Front St., 92188
(714) 293-6165

San Francisco:
Federal Bldg., Rm. 1001
450 Golden Ave., 94102
(415) 556-6667

Colorado
•Denver:
1845 Sherman St., 80203
(303) 837-3506

Connecticut
Hartford:
Federal Bldg., Rm. 717, 450 Main St., 06103
(203) 244-3096

Delaware
•Wilmington:
Federal Bldg., 844 King St., 19801
(302) 571-6288

District of Columbia
Metro Area:
1900 E Street, N.W., 20415
(202) 737-9616

Florida
•Miami:
330 Biscayne Blvd., Suite 410, 33131
(305) 350-4725

•Orlando:
80 N. Hughey Ave., 32801
(305) 420-6148

Georgia
Atlanta:
Richard B. Russell Federal Bldg.
75 Spring St. S.W., 30303
(404) 221-4315

Guam
Agana:
238 O'Hara St.
Room 308, 96910
344-5242

Hawaii
Honolulu (and Island of Oahu):
Federal Bldg. Room 1310
300 Ala Moana Blvd., 96850
(808) 546-7108

Illinois
Chicago:
Dirksen Bldg., Rm. 1322
219 S. Dearborn St., 60604
(312) 353-5136

Indiana
Indianapolis:
46 East Ohio Street, Rm. 123, 46204
(317) 269-7161 or 7162

Iowa
Des Moines:
210 Walnut St., Rm. 191, 50309
(515) 284-4546

Kansas
Wichita:
One-Twenty Bldg., Rm. 101
120 S. Market St., 67202
(316) 267-6311, ext. 106
In Johnson and Wyandott Counties dial
374-5702

Kentucky
Louisville:
Federal Building
600 Federal Pl., 40202
(502) 582-5130

Louisiana
New Orleans:
F. Edward Hebert Bldg.
610 South St., Rm. 103, 70130
(504) 589-2764

Maine
Augusta:
Federal Bldg., Rm. 611
Sewall St. & Western Ave., 04330
(207) 622-6171, ext. 269

Maryland
Baltimore:
Garmatz Federal Building
101 W. Lombard St., 21201
(301) 962-3822

D.C. Metro Area:
1900 E St., N.W., 20415
(202) 737-9616

Massachusetts
Boston:
3 Center Plaza, 02108
(617) 223-2571

Michigan
Detroit:
477 Michigan Ave., Rm. 595, 48226
(313) 226-6950

Minnesota
Twin Cities:
Federal Bldg.
Ft. Snelling, Twin Cities, 55111
(612) 725-3355

Mississippi
Jackson:
100 W. Capitol St. (Suite 335), 39201
(601) 490-4588

Missouri
Kansas City:
Federal Bldg., Rm. 129
601 E. 12th St., 64106
(816) 374-5702

St. Louis:
Federal Bldg., Rm. 1712
1520 Market St., 63103
(314) 425-4285

Montana
Helena:
Federal Bldg. & Courthouse
301 S. Park, Rm. 153, 59601
(406) 449-5388

Nebraska
Omaha:
U.S. Courthouse and Post Office Bldg.
Rm. 1014, 215 N. 17th St., 68102
(402) 221-3815

Nevada
• **Reno:**
Mill & S. Virginia Streets
P.O. Box 3296, 89505
(702) 784-5535

New Hampshire
Portsmouth:
Federal Bldg., Rm. 104
Daniel & Penhallow Streets, 03801
(603) 436-7720, ext. 762

New Jersey
Newark:
Federal Bldg., 970 Broad St., 07102
(201) 645-3673
In Camden, dial (215) 597-7440

New Mexico
Albuquerque:
Federal Bldg., 421 Gold Ave. S.W., 87102
(505) 766-2557

New York
Bronx:
590 Grand Concourse, 10451
(212) 292-4666

Buffalo:
111 W. Huron St., Rm. 35, 14202
(716) 846-4001

Jamaica:
90-04 161st St., Rm. 200, 11432
(212) 526-6192

New York City:
Federal Bldg., 26 Federal Plaza, 10278
(212) 264-0422

Syracuse:
100 S. Clinton St., 13260
(315) 423-5660

North Carolina
Raleigh:
Federal Bldg., 310 New Bern Ave.
P.O. Box 25069, 27611
(919) 755-4361

North Dakota
Fargo:
Federal Bldg., Rm. 202
657 Second Ave. N., 58102
(701) 237-5771, ext. 363

Ohio
Cleveland:
Federal Bldg., 1240 E. 9th St., 44199
(216) 522-4232

Dayton:
Federal Building Lobby
200 W. 2nd St., 45402
(513) 225-2720 and 2854

Oklahoma
Oklahoma City:
200 N.W. Fifth St., 73102
(405) 231-4948

Oregon
Portland:
Federal Bldg. Lobby (North)
1220 S.W. Third St., 97204
(503) 221-3141

Pennsylvania
•Harrisburg:
Federal Bldg., Rm. 168, 17108
(717) 782-4494

Philadelphia:
Wm. J. Green Jr. Fed. Bldg.
600 Arch Street, 19106
(215) 597-7440

Pittsburgh:
Fed. Bldg., 1000 Liberty Ave., 15222
(412) 644-2755

Puerto Rico
San Juan:
Federico Degetau Federal Bldg.
Carlos E. Chardon St.
Hato Rey, P.R. 00918
(809) 753-4209, ext. 209

Rhode Island
Providence:
Federal & P.O. Bldg., Rm. 310
Kennedy Plaza, 02903
(401) 528-4447

South Carolina
Charleston:
Federal Bldg., 334 Meeting St., 29403
(803) 724-4328

South Dakota
Rapid City:
Rm. 201, Federal Building
U.S. Court House, 515 9th St., 57701
(605) 348-2221

Tennessee
Memphis:
Federal Bldg., 167 N. Main St., 38103
(901) 521-3956

Texas
Dallas:
Rm. 1C42, 1100 Commerce St., 75242
(214) 767-8035

El Paso:
Property Trust Bldg., Suite N302
2211 E. Missouri Ave., 79903
(915) 543-7425

Houston:
701 San Jacinto St., 77002
(713) 226-5501

San Antonio:
643 E. Durango Blvd., 78205
(512) 229-6600

Utah

•**Salt Lake City:**
1234 South Main St., 2nd Floor, 84101
(801) 524-5744

Vermont

Burlington:
Federal Bldg., Rm. 614
P.O. Box 489
Elmwood Ave. & Pearl St., 05402
(802) 862-6712

Virginia

Norfolk:
Federal Bldg., Rm. 220
200 Granby Mall, 23510
(804) 441-3355

D.C. Metro Area:
1900 E Street N.W., 20415
(202) 737-9616

Washington

•**Seattle:**
Federal Bldg., 915 Second Ave., 98174
(206) 442-4365

West Virginia

•**Charleston:**
Federal Bldg., 500 Quarrier St., 25301
(304) 343-6181, ext. 226

Wisconsin

Milwaukee:
Plankinton Bldg., Rm. 205
161 W. Wisconsin Ave., 53203
(414) 244-3761

Wyoming

Cheyenne:
2120 Capitol Ave., Rm. 304
P.O. Box 967, 82001
(307) 778-2220, ext. 2108

Listing of Federal Personnel Offices in the Washington Metropolitan Area

Source:
United States Office of Personnel Management

Action

(Includes Foster Grandparents, Peace Corps, SCORE, VISTA)
806 Connecticut Avenue, N.W., Room 306
Washington, D.C. 20525

Administrative Office of the United States Courts

Personnel Division, Room 701
Washington, D.C. 20544 (202) 633-6116

Agency for International Development (AID)

Recruitment Staff
Room 111
515 22nd Street, N.W.
Washington, D.C. 20531 (202) 632-9062

Agriculture

Inquiries to offices in the South Building should be addressed as follows:
Department of Agriculture
(Agency)
Room_____, South Building
14th Street and Independence Ave., S.W.
Washington, D.C. 20250

Agricultural Marketing Service
Room 1721, South Building 447-4874

Agricultural Research Service
Room 569, Federal Center Building 1
Hyattsville, Maryland 20782 (301) 436-8116

Agricultural Research Service
Northeastern Region, Personnel Branch
Room 112, Building 003, ARC West
Beltsville, Maryland 20705 (301) 344-2700

Agricultural Stabilization and conservation Service
Room 4977, South Building 447-7517

Animal and Plant Inspection Service
Room 514, Pres. Building 436-6355

Economics, Statistics, and Cooperative Services
Room 1459, South Building 447-2244

Extension Service
Room 6446, South Building 447-5741

Farmers Home Administration
Room 6990, South Building 447-3025

Federal Crop Insurance Corporation
Room 4614, South Building 447-2766

Federal Grain Inspection Service
Room 1726, South Building 447-3967

Food and Nutrition Service
Room 711-A, GHI Building
500 12th Street, S.W.
Washington, D.C. 20250 447-8114

Food and Safety Quality Service
Room 3438, South Building 447-6617

**Office of Personnel
Personnel Operations Division**
(Services Office of Secretary)
Room 43-W, Administration Building
Washington, D.C. 20250 447-3764

Foreign Agricultural Service
Room 5627, South Building 447-2757

Forest Service
(Washington Area Only)
913 Rosslyn Plaza E
Arlington, Virginia 22209 (703) 235-2730

(Field Activities)
801 Rosslyn Plaza E
Arlington, Virginia 22209 (703) 235-2044

Rural Electrification Administration
Room 4072, South Building 447-3577

Soil Conservation Service
(Clerical) 6224 South Building 447-4264
(Other) 6227 South Building 447-2631

USDA Soil Conservation Service
4321 Hartwick Road, Room 522
College Park, Maryland 20740 (301) 344-4197

Air Force
Headquarters, 1947th AS/DMPK
Washington, D.C. 20330 (202) OX-79145

76 ABG/DPCR
Andrews Air Force Base
Washington, D.C. 20331

Appalachian Regional Commission
1666 Connecticut Avenue, N.W.
Washington, D.C. 20235

Army
Army Audit Agency, Civilian Personnel Office
Room 323, Nassif Building
5611 Columbia Pike
Falls Church, Virginia 22041 (703) 756-1980

**Harry Diamond Laboratories,
ATTN: DELHD-CP**
2800 Powder Mill Road, Room 1A002
Adelphi, Maryland 20783 (301) 394-2816

Material Development and Readiness Command
Darcom Building, Room 2F24
5001 Eisenhower Avenue
Alexandria, Virginia 22333 (703) 274-9446

Military District of Washington (5 locations)
Forrestal Placement Branch
Room 4F087, Forrestal Building
Washington, D.C. 20314 (202) 693-5327

Fort Myer Placement Branch
Building 305 North Fort Myer
Fort Myer, Virginia 22211 (703) 692-3220

Hoffman Placement Branch
Room 3N59 Hoffman Building 11
Alexandria, Virginia 22332 (703) 325-8840

Pentagon Placement Branch
Room 1A909 Pentagon Building
Washington, D.C. 20310 (202) 695-2690

MDW Civilian Personnel Directorate
Room 7218, 1900 Half Street, S.W.
Washington, D.C.

Army
Intelligence and Security Command
Arlington Hall Station
Arlington, Virginia 22212 (703) 692-5411

Personnel and Employment Service
Room 3D-727
Pentagon
Washington, D.C. 20310 (202) 697-0335

Recruitment and Placement Branch
Civilian Personnel Office, Building 498
Fort Belvoir, Virginia 22060 (703) 664-3874

Walter Reed Army Medical Center
Recruitment and Placement Division CPO
Building T-20, Room 213
Washington, D.C. 20012 (202) 576-3590

Civil Aeronautics Board
1875 Connecticut Avenue, Room 416
Washington, D.C. 20428

Commerce

Bureau of the Census
Room 3252, FB 3
Suitland, Maryland 20233

Employment Information Center
14th Street and Constitution Avenue, N.W.
Washington, D.C. 20230 (202) 377-4285

Industry and Trade Administration
Room 3512
14th Street and Constitution Avenue, N.W.
Washington, D.C. 20230 (202) 377-3301

Maritime Administration
Room 1091
14th Street and Constitution Avenue, N.W.
Washington, D.C. 20230

National Bureau of Standards
Administration Building, Room A123
Washington, D.C. 20234 (301) 921-3762

National Technical Information Service
Personnel Office, Room 1025, Sills Building
5285 Port Royal Road
Springfield, Virginia 22151

Office of the Secretary
Room 5014
14th Street and Constitution Avenue, N.W.
Washington, D.C. 20230

Patent and Trademark Office
Crystal Plaza, Building 2
Room 9C05
Jefferson Davis Highway
Arlington, Virginia 22202

Commodity Futures Trading Commission

Personnel Office
2033 K Street, N.W.
Washington, D.C. 20581

Community Services Administration

ABOLISHED IN 1981

Consumer Product Safety Commission

5401 Westbard Avenue, Room 956
Bethesda, Maryland 20207

Defense

Office of the Secretary, Directorate for Personnel
Room 3B47, Pentagon
Washington, D.C. 20301 (202) OX 7-9205

Uniformed Services University of the Health Services
4301 Jones Bridge Road
Bethesda, Maryland 20014 (301) 295-2180

Defense Communications Agency

Headquarters Office
Attn: Code 132
8th Street and South Courthouse Road
Arlington, Virginia 22204

Command and Control Technical Center (Pentagon)
Civilian Personnel Office (C130)
Room BF712, Pentagon
Washington, D.C. 20301 (202) 697-1071

Command and Control Technical Center
Civilian Personnel Office (C130R)
11440 Isaac Newton Square N.
Reston, Virginia 22090 (202) 437-2501

Defense Communications Engineering Center
(Reston)
Office (R130), Room 1A06A, Derey
Engineering Building
1860 Wiehele Avenue
Reston, Virginia 22090

Defense Contract Audit Agency

Civilian Personnel Division
Recruitment Branch, PM-1D
Washington, D.C. 20301 (202) 695-0920

Defense Investigative Service

Civilian Personnel Office, Room 2H086
D0151, Forrestal Building
1000 Independence Avenue, S.W.
Washington, D.C. 20314

Defense Mapping Agency

Headquarters, Defense Mapping Agency
Civilian Personnel Division, Room 206
Building 56, U.S. Naval Observatory
Washington, D.C. 20305

Hydrographic/Topographic Center
ATTN: 2000
6500 Brookes Lane
Washington, D.C. 20315

Defense Nuclear Agency

ATTN: PACV
Washington, D.C. 20305

Defense Logistics Agency

Civilian Personnel, DASC-ZE
Room 4D690, Cameron Station
Alexandria, Virginia 22314 (202) 274-7087/88

Department of Energy

Central Employment Office
20 Massachusetts Avenue, N.W.
Washington, D.C. 20545 (202) 376-4150

District of Columbia Government

Board of Education
Personnel Division, Room 706
415 12th Street, N.W.
Washington, D.C. 20004 (202) 724-4080

Central Personnel Office
499 Pennsylvania Avenue, N.W., Room 101
Washington, D.C. 20001 (202) 629-2848

D.C. General Hospital
Personnel Manpower Division
19th Street and Massachusetts Ave., S.E.
Washington, D.C. 20003

D.C. Superior Court
Personnel Division, Room 505
613 G Street, N.W.
Washington, D.C. 20001 (202) 727-1776

Department of Environmental Services
Personnel Division, Room 210
415 12th Street, N.W.
Washington, D.C. 20004 (202) 727-3098

Department of General Services
Personnel Division, Room 1014
613 G Street, N.W.
Washington, D.C. (202) 727-0126

**Department of Housing and Community
Development**
1325 G Street, N.W., Room 850
Washington, D.C. 20005

Department of Human Resources
Personnel Division, Room 300
801 North Capitol Street, N.E.
Washington, D.C. (202) 629-3503

Department of Recreation
Personnel Division
1320 Taylor Street, N.W.
Washington, D.C. 20005 (202) 576-6440

Department of Transportation
Personnel Division, Room 411
415 12th Street, N.W.
Washington, D.C. 20004 (202) 629-3155

Metropolitan Police Department
Personnel Division, Municipal Center
300 Indiana Avenue, N.W.
Washington, D.C. 20001 (202) 727-3098

Martin Luther King, Jr. Public Library
Personnel Division, Room 425
901 G Street, N.W.
Washington, D.C. 20004 (202) 727-1131

Environmental Protection Agency

Headquarters Personnel Office
401 M Street, S.W.
Washington, D.C. 20460 (202) 755-2506

National Employment Center
401 M Street, S.W.
Washington, D.C. 20460 (202) 755-0614

Equal Employment Opportunity Commission

2401 E Street, N.W., Room 3214
Washington, D.C. 20506 (202) 634-7040

Export-Import Bank of the United States

Room 1005, Lafayette Building
811 Vermont Avenue, N.W.
Washington, D.C. 20571 (202) 382-2078

Farm Credit Administration

4th Floor
490 L'Enfant Plaza East, S.W.
Washington, D.C. 20578

Federal Communications Commission

Room 208, 1919 M Street, N.W.
Washington, D.C. 20554

Federal Deposit Insurance Corporation

Room 800, 1709 New York Avenue, N.W.
Washington, D.C. 20429 (202) 389-4301

Federal Home Loan Bank Board

1700 G Street, N.W., 2nd Floor
Washington, D.C. 20552 (202) 377-6060

Federal Labor Relations Authority

1717 H Street, N.W.
Washington, D.C. 20415

Federal Maritime Commission

1100 L Street, N.W., Room 11213
Washington, D.C. 20573 (202) 523-5773

Federal Mediation and Conciliation Service

2100 K Street, N.W.
Washington, D.C. 20427

Federal Reserve Board

20th Street and Constitution Avenue, N.W.
Room B-1434
Washington, D.C. 20551 (202) 452-3880

Federal Trade Commission

6th Street and Pennsylvania Avenue, N.W.
Washington, D.C. 20580

Foreign Claims Settlement Commission
1111 20th Street, N.W., Room 417
Washington, D.C. 20579

General Accounting Office
Room 7536, 441 G Street, N.W.
Washington, D.C. 20548 (202) 275-6361

General Services Administration
Central Office: Room 1105
18th and F Streets, N.W.
Washington, D.C. 20425 (202) 566-0085

GSA Federal Preparedness Agency
Personnel Management Division
P.O. Box 464
Berryville, Virginia 22611
(202) 737-5721, Ext. 5521

Region 3: Personnel Division
Room 1030, 7th and D Streets, S.W.
Washington, D.C. 20407 (202) 472-1096

Government Printing Office
Room C104, North Capitol and H Sts., N.W.
Washington, D.C. 20401

Health and Human Services
Office of the Secretary
4348 HEW Building
330 Independence Avenue, S.W.
Washington, D.C. 20201 (202) 245-6851

Office of the Assistant Secretary for Health
17A-08 Parklawn Building
5600 Fishers Lane
Rockville, Maryland 20857 (301) 443-1986

Office of the Assistant Secretary for Education
345-G Humphrey Building
200 Independence Avenue, S.W.
Washington, D.C. 20201

Alcohol, Drug Abuse and Mental Health Administration
15C-24 Parklawn Building
5600 Fishers Lane
Rockville, Maryland 20857 (301) 443-4826

Bureau of Hearings and Appeals, SSA
205 IBM Building
3833 N. Fairfax Drive (Arlington)
P.O. Box 2518
Washington, D.C. 20013 (703) 235-8591

Food and Drug Administration
4B-10 Parklawn Building
5600 Fishers Lane
Rockville, Maryland 20857 (301) 443-1970

Health Care Financing Administration
2500 Switzer Building
330 C Street, S.W.
Washington, D.C. 20201 (202) 245-0614

Health Resources Administration
9-27 Center Building
3700 East-West Highway
Hyattsville, Maryland 20782 (301) 436-7244

Health Services Administration
12-27 Parklawn Building
5600 Fishers Lane
Rockville, Maryland 20857 (301) 443-6707

Department of Education
1102 F.O.B. No. 6
400 Maryland Avenue, S.W.
Washington, D.C. 20202 (202) 254-8404

National Institute of Education
642 Brown Building
1200 19th Street, N.W.
Washington, D.C. 20208 (202) 254-5450

National Institutes of Health
B3-C15 Building No. 31
9000 Rockville Pike
Bethesda, Maryland 20205 (301) 496-2403

Office of Human Development Services
347-D Humphrey Building
200 Independence Avenue, S.W.
Washington, D.C. 20201 (202) 245-2876

St. Elizabeth's Hospital, ADAMHA
Lobby; Building E
2700 M.L. King Jr., Avenue, S.E.
Washington, D.C. 20032 (202) 574-7452

Housing and Urban Development
Personnel Operations Division
451 7th Street, S.W.
Washington, D.C. 20410
Dial-A-Job (202) 755-3203

Inter-American Foundation
Personnel Office
1515 Wilson Boulevard
Rosslyn, Virginia 22209

Interior
Bureau of Indian Affairs
Room 334
1951 Constitution Avenue, N.W.
Washington, D.C. 20245 (202) 343-4841

Bureau of Land Management
Room 2038
18th and C Streets, N.W.
Washington, D.C. 20240 (202) 343-4251

Bureau of Reclamation
Room 7549
18th and C Streets, N.W.
Washington, D.C. 20240 (202) 343-5428

Bureau of Mines
5th Floor, Columbia Plaza
2401 E Street, N.W.
Washington, D.C. 20241

Employment Information Center
Room 2640
18th and C Streets, N.W.
Washington, D.C. 20240 (202) 343-2154

National Park Service
Room 2328
18th and C Streets, N.W.
Washington, D.C. 20240

National Park Service
National Capital Region
Room 224
1100 Ohio Drive, S.W.
Washington, D.C. 20242 (202) 426-6654

Office of the Secretary
Division of Personnel Services
Room 5459
18th and C Streets, N.W.
Washington, D.C. 20240

Office of the Solicitor
Room 6352
18th and C Streets, N.W.
Washington, D.C. 20240

Office of Surface Mining Reclamation and
Enforcement
Room 134
1951 Constitution Avenue, N.W.
Washington, D.C. 20245 (202) 343-4167

The Heritage Conservation and Recreation
Service
Room 326, Pension Building
440 G Street, N.W.
Washington, D.C. 20001 (202) 343-4275

U.S. Fish and Wildlife Service
Room 3452
18th and C Streets, N.W.
Washington, D.C. 20240 (202) 343-7742

U.S. Geological Survey
Room 1-A-315, MS 215
12201 Sunrise Valley Drive
Reston, Virginia 22092 (703) 860-6131

International Communications Agency
1776 Pennsylvania Avenue, N.W.
Washington, D.C. 20547

Interstate Commerce Commission
Room 1136
12th Street and Constitution Avenue, N.W.
Washington, D.C. 20423 (202) 275-7288

Justice
Bureau of Prisons
HOLC Building, Room 416
320 1st Street, N.W.
Washington, D.C. 20534

Drug Enforcement Administration
1405 I Street, N.W., Room 805-E
Washington, D.C. 20537 (202) 382-1219

Federal Bureau of Investigation
Hoover Building, Room 6052
9th Street and Pennsylvania Avenue, N.W.
Washington, D.C. 20530

Immigration and Naturalization Service
425 I Street, N.W., Room 6016
Washington, D.C. 20536

Law Enforcement Assistance Administration
Indiana Building, Room 1044
633 Indiana Avenue, N.W.
Washington, D.C. 20530

Employment Information Center
Department of Justice, Room 1264
10th Street and Pennsylvania Ave., N.W.
Washington, D.C. 20530 (202) 739-3121/22

United States Marshals Service
Personnel Management and Training
Division
One Tysons Corner Center, Room 231
McLean, Virginia 22102

Labor
Directorate of Personnel Management
Room S1318, 200 Constitution Avenue, N.W.
Washington, D.C. 20210 (202) 523-6255

Mine Health and Safety Administration
4015 Wilson Boulevard, Room 509
Arlington, Virginia 22203 (703) 235-1352

Library of Congress
Employment Office, Room G106B
10 First Street, S.E.
Washington, D.C. 20540 (202) 426-5620

Merit Systems Protection Board
1717 H Street, N.W.
Washington, D.C. 20415

National Aeronautics and Space Administration

Room 214, FOB No. 10
600 Independence Avenue, S.W.
Washington, D.C. 20546
(202) 755-3054 or 3363

Goddard Space Flight Center
Building 1, Room 145—Code 225
Greenbelt, Maryland 20771 (301) 982-5326

National Capital Housing Authority

Room 850, 1325 G Street, N.W.
Washington, D.C. 20430 (202) 724-2094

National Capital Planning Commission

Room 1079, 1325 G Street, N.W.
Washington, D.C. 20576 (202) 724-0178

National Credit Union Administration

2025 M Street, N.W., Room 3106
Washington, D.C. 20456

National Endowment for the Arts

Room W-711
2401 E Street, N.W.
Washington, D.C. 20506 (202) 632-4853

National Endowment for the Humanities

806 15th Street, N.W., Room 410
Washington, D.C. 20506

National Gallery of Art

Personnel Office
6th Street and Constitution Avenue, N.W.
Washington, D.C. 20565
(202) 737-4215, Ext. 311

National Labor Relations Board

Room 334, 1717 Pennsylvania Avenue, N.W.
Washington, D.C. 20570

National Mediation Board

ATTN: Personnel Office
Washington, D.C. 20550

National Science Foundation

Room 212, 1800 G Street, N.W.
Washington, D.C. 20550

National Security Agency

Director of Civilian Personnel
ATTN: M321
Ft. George G. Meade, Maryland 20755
(301) 796-6161

National Transportation Safety Board

800 Independence Avenue, S.W., Room 806
Washington, D.C. 20594 (202) 426-8932

Navy

Bureau of Medicine and Surgery
Civilian Personnel Office (0114)
Building 1—Room 1019
23rd and E Streets, N.W.
Washington, D.C. 20372 (202) 254-4122

Capital Area Personnel Services Office, Navy
Ballston Centre Two
801 N. Randolph Street
Arlington, Virginia 22203

Consolidated Civilian Personnel Office
Washington Navy Yard
Washington, D.C. 20374

Headquarters, U.S. Marine Corps
Arlington Navy Annex, Room 1107
Arlington, Virginia
Mailing Address: Civilian Personnel Branch
(HQSG), HQMC
Washington, D.C. 20380

Marine Corps Development and Education Command
Attn: Civilian Personnel Office
Quantico, Virginia 22134 (703) 640-2048

Military Sealift Command
4228 Wisconsin Avenue, N.W., Room 456
Washington, D.C. 20016 (202) 282-2882

National Naval Medical Center
Civilian Personnel Service, Building 123
Bethesda, Maryland 20014

Naval Air Systems Command
Civilian Personnel Division
Room 188, Jefferson Plaza 2
1421 Jefferson Davis Highway
Washington, D.C. 20361 (202) 692-8478

Naval Facilities Engineering Command
Chesapeake Division, Personnel Office
Building 108, Washington Navy Yard
Washington, D.C. 20374

Naval Ordnance Station
Civilian Personnel Department
Indian Head, Maryland 20640 (301) 743-4501

Naval Research Laboratory
4555 Overlook Avenue, S.W.
Washington, D.C. 20375 (202) 767-3030

Naval Sea Systems Command
CPO, Room 4E36, National Center 3
2531 S. Jefferson Davis Highway
Washington, D.C. 20362 (202) 692-1620

Naval Security Group Command, CPO
2801 Nebraska Avenue, N.W., Room 1120
Washington, D.C. 20390 (202) 282-0520

Naval Surface Weapons Center
White Oak Laboratory
Silver Spring, Maryland 20910 (301) 394-1700

Naval Supply Systems Command
Civilian Personnel Office
Crystal Mall No. 3, Room 817
Washington, D.C. 20376 (202) 697-0461

Office of Naval Research
Director of Civilian Personnel
Room 823, Ballston Tower No. 1
800 North Quincy Street
Arlington, Virginia 22217

Office of Management and Budget
New Executive Office Building
726 Jackson Place, N.W.
Washington, D.C. 20503

Office of Personnel Management
1900 E Street, N.W.
Room 1469
Washington, D.C. 20415 (202) 632-6291

Occupational Safety and Health Review Commission
Room 408, 1825 K Street, N.W.
Washington, D.C. 20006 (202) 282-0520

Overseas Private Investment Corporation
Personnel Office, 1129 20th Street, N.W.
Washington, D.C. 20527 (202) 632-8618

Pension Benefit Guaranty Corporation
2020 K Street, N.W., Room 6100
Washington, D.C. 20006 (202) 254-4779

Postal Rate Commission
Room 500, 2000 L Street, N.W.
Washington, D.C. 20268

Renegotiation Board
Office of Administration, Room 4306
2000 M Street, N.W.
Washington, D.C. 20446

Securities and Exchange Commission
Room 750, 500 N. Capitol Street, N.W.
Washington, D.C. 20549 (202) 755-1340

Selective Service System
National Headquarters: Administration and Logistics Division
600 E Street, N.W., 7th Floor
Washington, D.C. 20435

Small Business Administration
1441 L Street, N.W., Room 300
Washington, D.C. 20416 (202) 653-6504

Smithsonian Institution
900 Jefferson Drive, S.W., Room 1410
Washington, D.C. 20560 (202) 381-6545

State
Employment Information Office
Room 2815, 22nd and D Streets, N.W.
Washington, D.C. 20520 (202) 632-0581

Transportation
Central Employment Information Office
Room 2223, 400 7th Street, S.W., Nassif Building
Washington, D.C. 20590 (202) 426-2550

Office of the Secretary
Personnel Operations Division
Room 9401, 400 7th Street, S.W., Nassif Building
Washington, D.C. 20590 (202) 426-6933

Federal Aviation Administration
Personnel Management Operations Division
Room 512, 800 Independence Avenue, S.W.
Washington, D.C. 20591 (202) 426-3229

U.S. Coast Guard
Headquarters Civilian Personnel Branch
Room 8112, 400 7th Street, S.W., Nassif Building
Washington, D.C. 20590 (202) 426-2330

Federal Highway Administration
Personnel Operations Division
Room 4401, 400 7th Street, S.W., Nassif Building
Washington, D.C. 20590 (202) 426-0515

Federal Railroad Administration
Office of Personnel and Training
Room 5412, 400 7th Street, S.W., Nassif Building
Washington, D.C. 20590 (202) 426-9771

National Highway and Traffic Safety Administration
Office of Personnel Management
Room 5306, 400 7th Street, S.W., Nassif Building
Washington, D.C. 20590 (202) 426-1595

Urban Mass Transportation Administration
Office of Personnel
Room 4116, 400 7th Street, S.W., Nassif Building
Washington, D.C. 20590 (202) 755-8070

Treasury

Bureau of Alcohol, Tobacco and Firearms
1200 Pennsylvania Avenue, N.W.
Washington, D.C. 20226 (202) 566-7321

Bureau of Engraving and Printing
Room 106A, 14th and C Streets, S.W.
Washington, D.C. 20228 (202) 447-9840

Bureau of Government Financial Operations
Room 112, Treasury Annex No. 1
Madison Place and Pennsylvania Ave., N.W.
Washington, D.C. 20226

Bureau of the Mint
Personnel Division, Room 920 Warner Bldg.
501 13th Street, N.W.
Washington, D.C. 20220

Bureau of the Public Debt
13th and C Streets, N.W., Room 276
Washington, D.C. 20226 (202) 447-1407

Comptroller of the Currency
Human Resources Division
490 L'Enfant Plaza East, S.W.
Washington, D.C. 20219 (202) 447-1460

Internal Revenue Service
Room 1028, 1111 Constitution Avenue, N.W.
Washington, D.C. 20224 (202) 566-6117

Office of the Secretary: Personnel Office
Room 1330, Main Treasury
15th Street and Pennsylvania Ave., N.W.
Washington, D.C. 20220

U.S. Customs Service
1301 Constitution Avenue, N.W., Room 6124
Washington, D.C. 20229 (202) 566-2451

U.S. Savings Bond Division: Office of Personnel
Room 219, Vanguard Building
1111 20th Street, N.W.
Washington, D.C. 20226

U.S. Secret Service
1800 G Street, N.W., Room 941
Washington, D.C. 20223 (202) 634-5800

U.S. Arms Control Disarmament Agency (ACDA)

Recruitment Office
Room 5720
Washington, D.C. 20451 (202) 632-2034

U.S. Commission on Civil Rights

1121 Vermont Avenue, N.W., Room 507
Washington, D.C. 20425

U.S. Courts Administrative Office

Supreme Court Building
Washington, D.C. 20544 (202) 393-1640

U.S. International Trade Commission

701 E Street, N.W.
Washington, D.C. 20436 (202) 523-0183

U.S. Nuclear Regulatory Commission

Room LA-1220
7910 Woodmont Avenue
Bethesda, Maryland 20555 (301) 492-7900

U.S. Postal Service

475 L'Enfant Plaza West, S.W.
Washington, D.C. 20260
Attn: Office of Headquarters Personnel

U.S. Tax Court

Personnel Office, Room 146
400 Second Street, N.W.
Washington, D.C. 20217 (202) 376-2724

Veterans Administration

Central Office (055B)
810 Vermont Avenue, N.W.
Washington, D.C. 20420 (202) 389-2459

Veterans Administration Hospital
Room 1B-111, 50 Irving Street, N.W.
Washington, D.C. 20422 (202) 389-7545

Washington Regional Office: Room 9402
941 North Capitol Street, N.E.
Washington, D.C. 20421 (202) 275-1426

Pay schedule for federal white collar workers, October 1982.

PAY SCHEDULE FOR FEDERAL WHITE-COLLAR WORKERS

THE GENERAL SCHEDULE

GS	1	2	3	4	5	6	7	8	9	10
1	$8,676	$8,965	$9,254	$9,542	$9,831	$10,000	$10,286	$10,572	$10,585	$10,857
2	9,756	9,987	10,310	10,585	10,703	11,018	11,333	11,648	11,963	12,278
3	10,645	11,000	11,355	11,710	12,065	12,420	12,775	13,130	13,485	13,840
4	11,949	12,347	12,745	13,143	13,541	13,939	14,337	14,735	15,133	15,531
5	13,369	13,815	14,261	14,707	15,153	15,599	16,045	16,491	16,937	17,383
6	14,901	15,398	15,895	16,392	16,889	17,386	17,883	18,380	18,877	19,374
7	16,559	17,111	17,663	18,215	18,767	19,319	19,871	20,423	20,975	21,527
8	18,339	18,950	19,561	20,172	20,783	21,394	22,005	22,616	23,227	23,838
9	20,256	20,931	21,606	22,281	22,956	23,631	24,306	24,981	25,656	26,331
10	22,307	23,051	23,795	24,539	25,283	26,027	26,771	27,515	28,259	29,003
11	24,508	25,325	26,142	26,959	27,776	28,593	29,410	30,227	31,044	31,861
12	29,374	30,353	31,332	32,311	33,290	34,269	35,248	36,227	37,206	38,185
13	34,930	36,094	37,258	38,422	39,586	40,750	41,914	43,078	44,242	45,406
14	41,277	42,653	44,029	45,405	46,781	48,157	49,533	50,909	52,285	53,661
15	48,553	50,171	51,789	53,407	55,025	56,643	58,261	59,879	61,497	63,115
16	56,945	58,843	60,741	62,639	64,537	66,435	68,333	70,231	72,129	
17	66,708	68,932	71,156	73,380	75,604					
18	78,184									

NOTE: Notwithstanding the salary rates shown, the maximum rate of basic pay legally payable to employes under this schedule may not exceed the rate payable for level 5 of the Executive Schedule,, currently $57,500.

57

Block "A" is the standard space allowed for description of work. Block "B" is an example of expanded experience block. An alternative to using additional ruled lines is to attach plain paper on which to type description of work, but retain the information blocks at top and bottom for each position.

---

21 Experience Begin with current or most recent work or volunteer experience and work back. Account for periods of unemployment exceeding three months and your residence address at that time on the last line of the experience blocks in order of occurrence.

May inquiry be made of your present employer regarding your character, qualifications, and record of employment?
(A "NO" will not affect your consideration for employment opportunities except for Administrative Law Judge positions.)   ☐ YES   ☐ NO

A

Name and address of employer's organization (include ZIP Code, if known)	Dates employed (give month and year)	Average number of hours per week
	From To	
	Salary or earnings	Place of employment
	Beginning $ per	City
	Ending $ per	State

Exact title of your position	Name of immediate supervisor	Area Code Telephone Number	Number and kind of employees you supervised

Kind of business or organization (manufacturing, accounting, social services, etc.)	If Federal service, civilian or military: series, grade or rank, and date of last promotion	Your reason for wanting to leave

Description of work (Describe your specific duties, responsibilities and accomplishments in this job.):

For agency use (skill codes, etc.)

B

Name and address of employer's organization (include ZIP Code, if known)	Dates employed (give month and year)	Average number of hours per week
	From To	
	Salary or earnings	Place of employment
	Beginning $ per	City
	Ending $ per	State

Exact title of your position	Name of immediate supervisor	Area Code Telephone Number	Number and kind of employees you supervised

Kind of business or organization (manufacturing, accounting, social services, etc.)	If Federal service, civilian or military: series, grade or rank, and date of last promotion	Your reason for leaving

Description of work (Describe your specific duties, responsibilities and accomplishments in this job.):

For agency use (skill codes, etc.)

If you need additional experience blocks, use Standard Form 171-A or blank sheets of paper
SEE INSTRUCTION SHEET

Sample civil service examination announcement for computer specialists. Note: This is not a current announcement. It is presented here as a guide to assist you in analyzing your skills for a civil service examination in your chosen profession.

What the Jobs Are

Computer Specialist	GS-7 Through GS-12
Programer	GS-7 Through GS-12
Systems Analyst	GS-7 Through GS-12
Equipment Analyst	GS-7 Through GS-12

As a **COMPUTER PROGRAMER**, you need numerical and logical ability, along with the understanding of computer limitations, to convert the symbolic statement of a business problem into a detailed logical flow chart for coding into computer language. You might coordinate the programing of an entire operation, preparing written instructions for computer operators. From time to time, you would analyze, review, and rewrite programs in order to increase the efficiency of a computer operation or adapt it to new requirements.

As a **COMPUTER SYSTEMS ANALYST**, you would require a first-hand knowledge of programing, although the job doesn't usually involve specific programing techniques. Analysts are generally concerned with the orderly study of the collection, evaluation, and organization of information and with converting it into programable form. You would have to be able to foresee some of the specific problems posed in the programing processes, as well as some of the possible solutions to them. Increased sophistication of computer systems is placing more importance on a background of advanced mathematics for systems analysis.

As a **COMPUTER EQUIPMENT ANALYST**, you would apply an intensive knowledge of computer design and capacities to determine how computers are used to meet specific programing and overall application needs. Your job might involve the initial selection, updating or replacing of equipment; establishing standards for their selection; or establishing standards for the overall management and use of the equipment.

As a **COMPUTER SPECIALIST**, if you qualify in more than one area of the computer field, or have a unique background of highly specialized work, you can use your professional experience in a wide range of interesting work assignments which are less restricted in scope than specific jobs described above.

Where the Jobs Are

If you meet the requirements below, you may be referred for jobs with Federal agencies throughout the United States and overseas.

Qualifications Required

In order to be qualified for jobs described in this announcement, you must have actual computer training or experience.

GENERAL experience for all specializations is progressively responsible experience in administrative, technical, or investigative lines of work, computer console operation, or other similar work. Routine clerical experience is not qualifying.

SPECIALIZED experience for all specializations is any one or a combination of the following:
1. Management analysis work which has provided a broad background in the analysis of organizational and functional relationships, systems, workflow and procedures; in procedural and methods planning; or work simplification and management improvement.

Requirements for Programer Systems Analyst Equipment Analyst Computer Specialist	All Specializations				
	Grade	General Experience	Specialized Experience	Specific Experience	Total
	GS-7	3 years	½ year	½ year	4 years
	GS-9	3 years	1 year	1 year	5 years
	Systems Analyst				
	Grade	General Experience	Specialized Experience	Specific Experience	Total
	GS-11/12	3 years	2 years	1 year	6 years
	Programer • Equipment Analyst • Computer Specialist				
	Grade	General Experience	Specialized Experience	Specific Experience	Total
	GS-11/12	3 years	1 year	2 years	6 years

2. Technical, analytical, supervisory, or administrative experience in a subject-matter field which has demonstrated, in addition to subject-matter knowledges, ability to deal analytically and systematically with problems of organization, workflow, analysis of information requirements, and planning of integrated procedural systems.
3. Experience in tabulation project planning which has involved development of data processing systems and has demonstrated experience in systems design, even though such positions have not functioned within a digital computer framework.
4. Experience in any occupation which has demonstrated ability to analyze and organize work processes or problems into plans for computer solutions, or ability to participate in the analysis of system and digital computer equipment requirements.

SPECIFIC EXPERIENCE

Computer Programer: Experience which demonstrates proficiency in developing computer programs, formats, and structures, skill in using programing principles and techniques at the level required in the specific positions, and the ability to apply sound judgment in analyzing and organizing problems or work processes for computer solution.

Computer Systems Analyst: Experience in the analysis of system requirements, of computer applications, or of basic plans for the processing of data by digital computers. Included is experience as a programer which has demonstrated both a knowledge of the substantive problems and work processes entailed in subject-matter applications, as well as skills required in the planning and design of segments of data processing programs and systems.

Computer Equipment Analyst: Experience may consist of:
1. Experience in any of the computer specializations which has required (a) an evaluation of computer characteristics and capabilities leading to the selection of equipment, the development of descriptions of equipment specifications, or statements of the equipment capabilities and capacities required; or (b) evaluation of the need for modification of equipment characteristics or capabilities. OR
2. Experience as a representative of a computer manufacturer in a customer service capacity (for example, as a systems engineer or a maintenance consultant) which has provided an intensive knowledge of the design features, capabilities, or capacities of digital computer equipment, as well as a knowledge of the nature of the types of applications for which equipment is best suited.

Computer Specialist: Experience which meets any of the specific experience requirements described above for the particular combination of specialties involved; or experience which demonstrates the ability to perform highly specialized tasks not totally identified with the above specializations.

IN ADDITION, experience as a computer console operator may be accepted as specific experience for programer positions or as specialized experience for the other specializations depending upon the specific duties performed and the knowledges and training required.

SUBSTITUTIONS FOR EXPERIENCE

1. Undergraduate study at an accredited college or university may be substituted for general experience at the rate of 1 academic year of study for 9 months of experience up to 4 years of such study for 3 years of general experience.
2. One full academic year of graduate education which included at least 12 semester hours in computer science may be substituted for all of the requirements for GS-7.
3. A bachelor's degree with a major in computer science which included at least 24 semester hours in computer science courses may be substituted for all the requirements for GS-7 under one of the following:
   (a) A 2.90 grade-point average on a 4.0 scale for all courses completed: (1) at the time of application; or (2) during the last 2 years of the undergraduate curriculum.
   (b) A 3.5 grade-point average in all computer science courses: (1) at the time of application; or (2) during the last 2 years of the undergraduate curriculum.
   (c) A standing in upper third of the college class or major subdivision.
   (d) Election to membership in one of the national honorary societies (other than freshman or sophomore societies) recognized by the Association of College Honor Societies.
4. Completion of all the requirements for a master's or an equivalent degree or 2 full academic years of graduate study which included at least 12 semester hours in computer science may be substituted for all of the requirements for grade GS-9.

Quality of Experience

Eligibility in any grade will be based on clear evidence that the applicant has experience which is sufficient in scope and quality to perform the level of assignments required of the position. NOTE: Excess specialized or specific experience may be applied to general experience requirements. Excess specific experience may also be applied to specialized experience requirements.

How to Apply

What

1. Personal Qualifications Statement, SF-171
2. Supplemental Qualifications Statement, CSC Form 1170/4
3. College transcripts or List of College Courses, CSC Form 226 or 1170/17
4. Card Form 5001-ABC
5. Standard Form 15 and required documentary proof if you are claiming 10-point veteran preference

Where

Mail application forms to the one Area Office maintaining the list of eligibles for the geographic area where you most want to work. (See below) File a copy of your notice of rating and a second qualifications statement with the Area Office for Washington, D.C., if you also wish to be considered for jobs there. You will receive primary consideration at these locations. In addition, you will automatically receive secondary consideration for jobs in other areas where you are available in the absence of qualified candidates on the appropriate lists of eligibles.

Location of Lists:

Lists of eligibles will be maintained at the following locations for the geographic areas shown. Send the required application forms to the **Area Office of the Office of Personnel Management** which has jurisdiction over your primary area of interest.

Southerland Building
806 Governors Drive, S.W.
HUNTSVILLE ALABAMA 35801

Alabama; Florida; Georgia; Kentucky (except Boyd, Henderson, Boone, Campbell, and Kenton Counties—see Pittsburgh, Detroit, and Dayton); Mississippi; North Carolina; South Carolina; Tennessee; Crittenden County, Arkansas; Floyd and Clark Counties, Indiana.

Federal Building
450 Main Street
HARTFORD, CONNECTICUT 06103

Connecticut; Maine; Massachusetts; New Hampshire; Rhode Island; Vermont.

Room 1322
219 South Dearborn Street
CHICAGO, ILLINOIS 60604

Illinois (except Madison and St. Clair Counties —see Kansas City); Minnesota (except Clay County—see Denver); Wisconsin; Scott County, Iowa.

200 West Second Street
DAYTON, OHIO 45402

Ohio (except Belmont, Jefferson, and Lawrence Counties—see Pittsburgh); Boone, Campbell, and Kenton Counties, Kentucky.

477 Michigan Avenue
Room 565
DETROIT, MICHIGAN 48226

Indiana (except Floyd and Clark Counties—see Huntsville); Michigan; Henderson County, Kentucky.

421 Gold Avenue, S.W.
ALBUQUERQUE, NEW MEXICO 87101

Arkansas (except Crittenden County—see Huntsville); Louisiana; New Mexico; Oklahoma; Texas.

1845 Sherman Street
DENVER, COLORADO 80203

Colorado; Montana; North Dakota; South Dakota; Utah; Wyoming; Clay County, Minnesota.

100 South Clinton Street
Room 843
SYRACUSE, NEW YORK 13260

New York; New Jersey (except Camden County—see Philadelphia); Puerto Rico; Virgin Islands.

Federal Building
101 West Lombard Street
BALTIMORE, MARYLAND 21201

Maryland (except Montgomery, Prince Georges, and Charles Counties—see Washington, D.C.).

Atlantic National Bank Building
415 St. Paul Boulevard
NORFOLK, VIRGINIA 23510

Virginia (except Arlington, Fairfax, Loudoun, Stafford, Prince William, and King George Counties, Falls Church, Fairfax City—see Washington, D.C.).

William J. Green, Jr. Federal Building
600 Arch Street
PHILADELPHIA, PENNSYLVANIA 19106
Delaware; Eastern Pennsylvania; Camden County, New Jersey.

Federal Building
1000 Liberty Avenue
PITTSBURGH, PENNSYLVANIA 15222
Central and Western Pennsylvania; West Virginia; Belmont, Jefferson, and Lawrence Counties, Ohio; Boyd County, Kentucky.

Room 129, Federal Building
601 East 12th Street
KANSAS CITY, MISSOURI 64106
Iowa (except Scott County—see Chicago); Kansas; Missouri; Nebraska; Madison and St. Clair Counties, Illinois.

Federal Building
300 Ala Moana Boulevard
P.O. Box 50028
HONOLULU, HAWAII 96850
Hawaii; Guam; Pacific Ocean area.

880 Front Street
SAN DIEGO, CALIFORNIA 92101
California; Arizona; Nevada.

Federal Building
Room 376
1220 Southwest Third Avenue
PORTLAND, OREGON 97204
Alaska; Idaho; Oregon; Washington.

1900 E Street, N.W.
WASHINGTON, D.C. 20415
District of Columbia; Charles, Montgomery, and Prince Georges Counties, Maryland; Arlington, Fairfax, Loudoun, Stafford, Prince William, and King George Counties, and Fairfax and Falls Church, Virginia; overseas areas except Pacific Ocean area.

General Information

Term of Eligibility

If you are found qualified, your name will go on a list with other qualified applicants and may be referred to Federal agencies having vacancies to be filled in the specialties described in this announcement; you may be referred for other closely related jobs as well. Your name will stay on the list for 1 year unless you accept a job or fail to reply to correspondence, or the list is terminated. If you want to stay on the list beyond that time, you should submit an updated Personal Qualifications Statement (SF 171) and a new Supplemental Qualifications Statement (CSC Form 1170/4) after 10, but no more than 12, months from the date on your notice of rating.

Basis of Rating

A written test is not required. You will be rated on the basis of your experience and education as described on your application forms.

Equal Employment Opportunity

All qualified applicants will receive consideration for appointment without regard to race, religion, color, national origin, sex, age, handicap, political affiliation or any other non-merit factor.

Additional Information

Information about citizenship, salaries, physical requirements, kinds of appointments, veteran preference and other general subjects, in addition to the forms you need to apply, can be obtained from Federal Job Information Centers. FJICs are listed in major metropolitan area telephone directories under "U.S. Government".

What About Trainee Positions?

Positions filled from this announcement require actual computer experience or training. However, each year the Federal government hires many trainees who have no specific computer experience or education for careers in the computer field.

The Professional and Administrative Career Examination (PACE), Announcement No. 429, is used to fill positions in a variety of occupations at the GS-5 and GS-7 levels. Most trainee positions in the computer field will be filled from PACE. Your local Federal Job Information Center can provide information on qualifications; a written test is required.

Computer Operator and Technician positions, GS-4 through GS-7, and other positions in the computer field at the GS-4 level are filled by local Office of Personnel Management Area Offices. Applicants must meet the qualifications outlined in the appropriate local announcements, which are available at Federal Job Information Centers.

The following pages contain examples of amendments to civil service examination announcements for accountants, auditors, computer specialists, life sciences, and nurses.

These amendments, issued quarterly, indicate areas of the United States where positions are to be filled. They change periodically. Interested applicants should check with the nearest OPM regional office for current information before applying.

Amendment to Announcement No. 425
ACCOUNTANTS, AUDITORS
Effective through March 31, 1983

OFFICE OF PERSONNEL MANAGEMENT
WASHINGTON, D.C. 20415

1. Effective January 1, 1983, only those Office of Personnel Management area offices listed below will accept applications under Announcement No. 425. The receipt of applications in other offices is suspended until further notice. Limitations, if any, on the specialties, grades, geographic locations, and filing dates are given for each office below:

Anchorage Area Office. Accountant/Auditor, GS-11/12, from February 1 through 28, only.

Atlanta Area Office. Accountant/Auditor, GS-11/12, from February 1 through 28, only.

Boston Area Office. Accountant/Auditor, GS-5/12, from March 1 through 31, only.

Denver Area Office. Accountant/Auditor, GS-5/12, from January 3 through February 11, only.

San Francisco Area Office. Accountant/Auditor, GS-11/12 for the entire quarter. Open for GS-5/7 DOD positions in Arizona, Nevada and California only from January 3 through February 28. NOTE: See paragraph 4, below.

Seattle Area Office. Accountant/Auditor GS-5/12 from March 21 through 31, only. NOTE: See paragraph 3, below.

2. The current edition of Announcement No. 425 is dated August 1982. The July 1981 edition may also be used.

3. The OPM examining office for the Northwest Region (Idaho, Oregon and Washington) has been changed from Portland to Seattle. The address of the Seattle office is: Federal Building, Room 2552, 915 Second Avenue, Seattle, WA 98174.

4. The address listed in the announcement for the Denver and San Francisco Area Offices are incorrect. The correct addresses are: 1845 Sherman Street, Denver, CO 80203 and P.O. Box 7405, San Francisco, CA 94120.

5. Auditors jobs at grades GS-5 and 7 in the Offices of the Inspectors General in various Federal agencies will not be filled through this announcement. Instead, these jobs will be announced locally in OPM Area Offices as needs arise.

6. The Office of Personnel Management has authorized a number of agencies to maintain their own lists of eligibles for filling their Accountant, Auditor and IRS Agent positions formerly filled from Announcement No. 425. The agencies to which we have delegated examining authority on a nationwide basis, along with information on the jobs covered and how and where to apply are listed on page 6 of the announcement. Other delegations at the higher grades (GS-9 and above) may exist in some locations. Information about them will be available at local Federal Job Information Centers (FJIC's).

7. THIS AMENDMENT SUPERSEDES AND CANCELS ALL PREVIOUS AMENDMENTS TO ANNOUNCEMENT NO. 425. This amendment is effective through March 31, 1983, at which time a revised amendment will be issued.

Amendment to Announcement No. 420
COMPUTER SPECIALIST
Effective through July 26, 1982
Issued July 1, 1982

OFFICE OF PERSONNEL MANAGEMENT
WASHINGTON, D.C. 20415

Nationwide coverage of Computer Specialist positions at grades GS-7 through GS-12 under Announcement No. 420 will terminate July 26, 1982. After that date each U.S. Office of Personnel Management regional office will provide local publicity and examination coverage for Computer Specialist positions, and examination coverage will be expanded to include GS-5.

A new examination has been developed which will cover entry level computer specialist trainee positions at grades GS-5 and GS-7. Ratings under the new examination will be based on a combination of a written test battery and an evaluation of computer specialist related education, training and experience. Applications to take the new test will be accepted during the period August 2 through 27, 1982; the test will be given during September 1982, and successful competitors will begin receiving employment consideration under the new examination around November 15, 1982. At that time, all GS-7 eligibilities established under Announcement No. 420 will be terminated.

To apply under the new Computer Specialist Trainee examination for consideration beginning in November 1982, file OPM Form 5000-AB with the OPM office having jurisdiction over the location where you wish to be tested. Federal Job Information Centers can provide the necessary forms and instructions.

Computer Specialist, GS-7

There is a current need for GS-7 Computer Specialists in some locations; therefore, the offices listed below will continue to accept applications for GS-7 under Announcement No. 420 during the period July 1 through *September 30, 1982*. Applicants who file under Announcement No. 420 during this period who wish also to be considered for GS-5/7 Computer Specialist positions after November 15 must also file during the August 2-27 open period and take and pass the written test. To apply to these offices for consideration through November 15, follow the application procedures given in Announcement No. 420.

> Baltimore Area Office—All options, GS-7
> Philadelphia Area Office—Programmer, Systems Analyst, Specialist, GS-7
> Pittsburgh Area Office—All options, GS-7
> Portland Area Office—All options, GS-7 for jobs in Portland, Oregon, only
> San Diego Area Office—All options, GS-7

Computer Specialist, GS-9/12

The offices listed below will accept applications for the specialties, grades and geographic locations indicated for the period July 1 through 26, 1982. After July 26, regional offices will issue local publicity about openings. The application and examining procedures for GS-9/12 computer specialist positions will remain the same and eligibilities established under Announcement No. 420 will continue under the local examination.

Albuquerque Area Office—All options, GS-9/12, for Oklahoma, Louisiana and the San Antonio, TX, area only.

Baltimore Area Office—All options, GS-9/12

Dayton Area Office—Programmer, Specialist, Systems Analyst, GS-9/12

Denver Area Office—Programmer, GS-9/11; Specialist, GS-9/11/12; Equipment Analyst, GS-11 for the State of Colorado only.

Detroit Area Office—All options, GS-9/12

Chicago Area Office—All options, GS-9/12, for Illinois, Minnesota and Wisconsin only

Hartford Area Office—All options, GS-9/12

Huntsville Area Office—All options, GS-9/12

Kansas City Area Office—All options, GS-9/12

Philadelphia Area Office—Programmer, Specialist, Systems Analyst, GS-9/12

Pittsburgh Area Office—All options, GS-9/12

Portland Area Office—All options, GS-9/12, for jobs in Portland, Oregon, only.

San Diego Area Office—All options, GS-9/12

Syracuse Area Office—All options, GS-9/12

Washington Area Office—All options, GS-9/12

Amendment to Announcement No. 421
LIFE SCIENCES
Effective through September 30, 1982

OFFICE OF PERSONNEL MANAGEMENT
WASHINGTON, D.C. 20415

1. Effective July 1, 1982, applications under Announcement No. 421 will be accepted for the following positions only:

Washington Area Office	Microbiologist, GS-9/12, from July 1-23, only. NOTE: Be sure to submit Supplemental Qualifications Statement for Life Sciences positions, OPM Form 1170/24.

USDA, Farmers Home Administration Special Examining Unit.	Agricultural Management, GS-5/5, nationwide except Hawaii and the Pacific Overseas area.
USDA, Soil Conservation Service Special Examining Unit.	Soil Conservation, GS-5/7, nationwide except Hawaii and the Pacific overseas area.
	Soil Science, GS-5/7, nationwide except Hawaii and the Pacific overseas area.
	Range Conservation, GS-5/7, nationwide except Hawaii and the Pacific overseas area.

NOTE: The addresses of these special examining units have changed to:

| USDA, Farmers Home Administration Special Examining Unit Personnel Division 6525 Belcrest Road Hyattsville, MD 20782 | USDA, Soil Conservation Service Special Examining Unit 10000 Aerospace Road Lanham, MD 20801 |

2. For information on jobs in Hawaii and the Pacific overseas area, contact the Honolulu Area Office, Prince Kuhio Federal Building, 300 Ala Moana Boulevard, P.O. Box 50028, Honolulu, Hawaii, 96850.

3. The current edition of Announcement No. 421 is dated October 1980 and is printed in blue type on white paper. The January, 1980, edition may also be used.

4. The coursework requirements for Range Conservation shown on page 3 of the January 1980, announcement have been changed. The new requirements, which appear in the October 1980, edition of the announcement, are: 42 semester hours in a combination of plant, animal and soil sciences and natural resources management with at least 18 semester hours in range management; 15 semester hours in directly related Plant, Animal and Soil Sciences (with at least one course in Plant Sciences, one course in Animal Sciences, and one course in Soil Sciences); and at least 9 semester hours in Natural Resources Management.

5. THIS AMENDMENT SUPERSEDES AND CANCELS ALL PREVIOUS AMENDMENTS TO ANNOUNCEMENT NO. 421. This amendment is effective through September 30, 1982, at which time a revised amendment will be issued.

Amendment to Announcement No. 419
NURSES
Effective through June 30, 1982

OFFICE OF PERSONNEL MANAGEMENT
WASHINGTON, D.C. 20415

1. Effective April 1, 1982, the following area offices will accept applications for professional nursing positions for the grades, options and time periods shown below. Unless otherwise noted, applications are accepted for all locations under the area offices jurisdictions.

Raleigh Area Office—Open for GS-9 only for all options and locations, for the entire quarter.

Hartford Area Office—Open for all covered grades and options for the entire quarter.

Dayton Area Office—Open for Nurse GS-7; Clinical and Occupational Health Nurse GS-9, for the entire quarter.

Philadelphia Area Office—Open for GS-7/9 Clinical and Occupational Health Nurse only.

St. Louis Area Office—Open for the entire quarter for all covered options at GS-5/7/9, and for GS-4 only at the Winnebago Indian Reservations, Winnebago, NE.

*San Diego Area Office—Open for the entire quarter for all covered options at GS-5/7/9, and for GS-4 only at the Navajo-Hopi Indian Reservation in Arizona and New Mexico.

New Orleans Area Office—Open for all covered grades and options for the entire quarter. Note: excellent opportunities at all grades at Indian Health Service facilities in Oklahoma. For information, contact Personnel Branch, Oklahoma City Area Indian Health Service, 388 Old Post Office and Courthouse Bldg; Oklahoma City, OK 73102, phone (405) 231-5581.

*Denver Area Office—Open for all covered grades and options for the entire quarter.

Syracuse Area Office—Open for GS-5 General Nurse and GS-5/7 Clinical and Occupational Health Nurse for the entire quarter.

Seattle Area Office—Open for GS-7/9 Clinical, Community Health, Occupational Health, Operating Room and Psychiatric Nurse for the entire quarter.

Washington Area Office—Open for all covered options and grades for the entire quarter.

Anchorage Area Office—Open for GS-4 Nurse between April 1 and May 14 only. Open for GS-5 Nurse and GS-7/9 Clinical, Operating Room, Psychiatric, Occupational Health, and Community Health Nurse for the entire quarter.

Honolulu Area Office—Open for GS-9 Clinical, Operating Room, Occupational Health, and Psychiatric Nurse for the entire quarter.

*NOTE: The San Diego, Denver and Washington Area Offices have given a number of agencies the authority to make direct appointments to certain nursing positions. For specific information on the agencies and positions involved, contact the area office.

2. Note carefully the examining jurisdictions described on pages 4-5 of Announcement 419. Not all nursing specialties are typically found at all grade levels; for example, Nurse Anesthetist, Nurse Midwife and Nurse Practitioner positions occur only at GS-9 and above, and Nurse Consultant, Nurse Educator, and Nurse Specialist positions occur only at GS-11 and above.

3. Announcement No. 419 for Nurses was revised and new rating procedures are in effect for Nurse, GS-4/5 and Clinical, Community Health, Occupational Health, Operating Room and Psychiatric Nurse GS-7/9. The current announcement is dated September 1981, and is maroon and white. All previous editions of Announcement No. 419 are obsolete. The Supplemental Qualifications Statement for Professional Nursing Positions, OPM Form 1170/10 has also been changed. The current edition is dated June 1981, and all previous editions of OPM Form 1170/10 are obsolete.

4. There are special higher pay rates for some nursing positions in Alaska, New York City, New Orleans, and the Boston, Washington, Baltimore, and San Francisco/Oakland metropolitan areas. Leaflet AN-2500 "Federal Government Entrance Salaries," gives details, and is available at Federal Job Information Centers.

5. THIS AMENDMENT SUPERSEDES AND CANCELS ALL PREVIOUS AMENDMENTS TO ANNOUNCEMENT NO. 419. This amendment is effective through June 30, 1982, at which time a revised amendment will be issued.

The following pages contain examination announcements in the fields of mathematics-related fields, physical sciences, engineering, and life sciences. They are presented for your guidance. They indicate how to apply, where positions are located, and employment opportunities in each field. These change periodically. Interested applicants should check with the nearest OPM regional office before applying.

Mathematics/Related Competition Notice

Effective Period: April 1 through June 30, 1982.

Employment opportunities vary by specialties and locales.

Qualifications Information Statement for Mathematics and Related Positions (QI-1500) provides information on the specialties covered and the qualifications required.

Two Ways to Apply

☐ To U.S. Office of Personnel Management (OPM) area offices: To apply through an automated competitor referral system, mail the forms in the "Federal Employment Application Instructions and Forms" booklet (OPM Form 1282) and the Occupational Supplement for Mathematicians and Related Positions (OPM Form 1203-L) to the office which serves the zone where you are interested in working. You may apply for consideration in more than one zone. However, this will require submitting separate application forms to each zone. Except for OPM Form 1203-L, which must be an original, application forms may be photocopied. Forms are available in all Federal Job Information Centers.

☐ To Federal agencies: Contact the Federal Job Information Center in the area where you seek employment for information about where to apply.

How Positions Are Filled

Some agencies use OPM's competitor inventories. Others do their own recruiting. Many agencies use both methods.

Once eligibility has been established with an office that maintains a competitor inventory, the highest ranked candidates are automatically referred to agencies as vacancies occur. Information about relative opportunities for placement through OPM inventories is provided in this Notice. Federal agencies maintaining their own inventories for positions in more than one zone are also noted. Federal Job Information Centers within the respective zones have information about any other agency inventories which are open for applications.

The OPM competitor inventories may or may not be used by agencies in filling positions at grade GS-9 and above. When they are not used, and the agency does not maintain its own inventories, individual vacancies are publicized directly by the hiring office or an OPM area office. For information about these opportunities, contact the Federal Job Information Center in the area where you want to work.

Federal Agencies Maintaining Separate Competitor Inventories

National Aeronautics and Space Administration (NASA): Aerospace Technologist positions GS-7/15 for all locations are recruited directly by NASA. Applicants should file with the NASA installation where they wish to work. Contact any Federal Job Information Center or NASA facility for a list of installations and addresses.

 United States Office of Personnel Management

Mathematics/ Related

Employment Prospects

Occupational Specialty	Grade Group	Alaska	Atlanta	Boston	Caribbean	Chicago	Dallas	Denver	New York	Philadelphia	St. Louis	San Francisco	Seattle	Washington, D.C.
Actuary	5/7					D			C		D			D
	9					D			D		D			D
	11/12					D			D		D			D
	13/15					D			D		D			D
Computer Scientist	5/7	B*	A*		A*	D	D	A		B	D	A	B	B
	9	B*	A		B*	D	D	A		B	D	B*	B	A
	11/12	A	A			D	D	A		C	D	C*	B	A
	13/15	D				D	D	D		D		D		A
Mathematician	5/7	D			C	B	B	C		B	D	C*	B	C
	9	C*			C	C	B	D	D	C	D	C*	B	B
	11/12	B*			C	D	C	D	D	D	D	C*	B	B
	13/15	D				D	D	D		D		B		B
Mathematical Statistician	5/7	D			D	C	D			B	D	C	B	C
	9	D			D	D	D		D	C	D	D	B	B
	11/12	D			D	D	D		D	D	D	D	C	B
	13/15	D				D	D			D		D		B
Operations Research Analyst	5/7	B*	B		B	C	C	C		B	C*	C	C	C
	9	A*	B		B	C	C	A	D	B	C*	D	C	B
	11/12	A*	B		C	C	D	B	D	B	B*	D	C	B
	13/15	D				D	D	D		D		D		B
Statistician	5/7	D			D	C	B	D		B	C	C	B	C
	9	D			D	D	C	D		C	C	D	B	B
	11/12	D			D	D	C	D		C	D	C	C	B
	13/15	D				D	D	D		D		D		C

Entrance Salaries:

GS-5	$12,854
GS-7	15,922
GS-9	19,477
GS-11	23,566
GS-12	28,245
GS-13	33,586
GS-14	39,689
GS-15	46,685

*Agencies/establishments may make immediate offers of employment for certain duty locations. Contact the area office in the zone for information.

Opportunity Codes (Subject to Change)

A. Excellent— Most qualified applicants receive job offers.
B. Good— Most well-qualified applicants receive job offers.
C. Fair— Some well-qualified applicants receive job offers.
D. Poor— Only a few of the best qualified applicants receive job offers.
No entry—(Limited). For specialties at grades GS-5/7, applications are not being accepted (unanticipated recruitment needs will be publicized locally). For specialties at grades GS-9 and above, the acceptance of applications, if needed, will be publicized locally.

Where to Apply

Zones/OPM Area Office Addresses

Alaska
Anchorage Area Office
Federal Bldg. & U.S. Courthouse
701 "C" Street, Box 22
Anchorage, Alaska 99513

Atlanta
Huntsville Area Office
Southerland Building
806 Governors Drive, S.W.
Huntsville, Alabama 35801

Boston
Boston Area Office
3 Center Plaza
Boston, Massachusetts 02108

Caribbean
Newark Area Office
970 Broad Street
Newark, New Jersey 07102

Chicago
Dayton Area Office
200 W. 2nd Street, Room 507
Dayton, Ohio 45402

Dallas
Oklahoma City Area Office
200 N.W. 5th Street, Room 205
Oklahoma City, Oklahoma 73102

Denver
Denver Area Office
1845 Sherman Street
Denver, Colorado 80203

New York
Newark Area Office
970 Broad Street
Newark, New Jersey 07102

Pacific
Honolulu Area Office
300 Ala Moana Blvd.,
P.O. Box 50028
Honolulu, Hawaii 96850

Philadelphia
Philadelphia Area Office
600 Arch Street
Philadelphia, Pennsylvania 19106

San Francisco
Los Angeles Area Office
845 S. Figueroa, 3rd Fl.
Los Angeles, California 90017

Seattle
Seattle Area Office
915 2nd Avenue, Room 2563
Seattle, Washington 98174

St. Louis
St. Louis Area Office
1520 Market Street
St. Louis, Missouri 63103

Washington, D.C.
Washington Area Office
1900 E Street, N.W.
Washington, D.C. 20415

U.S. GOVERNMENT PRINTING OFFICE: 1982-361-390:110

U.S. GOVERNMENT PRINTING OFFICE: 1982-361-390:113

Physical Sciences Competition Notice

Effective Period: April 1 through June 30, 1982.

Employment opportunities vary by specialties and locales.

Qualifications Information Statement for Physical Sciences Positions (QI-1300) provides information on the specialties covered and the qualifications required.

Two Ways to Apply

☐ To U.S. Office of Personnel Management (OPM) area offices: To apply through an automated competitor referral system, mail the forms in the "Federal Employment Application Instructions and Forms" booklet (OPM Form 1282) and the Occupational Supplement for Physical Sciences Positions (OPM Form 1203-K) to the office which serves the zone where you are interested in working. You may apply for consideration in more than one zone. However, this will require submitting separate application forms to each zone. Except for OPM Form 1203-K, which must be an original, application forms may be photocopied. Forms are available in all Federal Job Information Centers

☐ To Federal agencies: Contact the Federal Job Information Center in the area where you seek employment for information about where to apply.

How Positions Are Filled

Some agencies use OPM's competitor inventories. Others do their own recruiting. Many agencies use both methods.

Once eligibility has been established with an office that maintains a competitor inventory, the highest ranked candidates are automatically referred to agencies as vacancies occur. Information about relative opportunities for placement through OPM inventories is provided in this Notice. Federal agencies maintaining their own inventories for positions in more than one zone are also noted. Federal Job Information Centers within the respective zones have information about any other agency inventories which are open for applications.

The OPM competitor inventories may or may not be used by agencies in filling positions at grade GS-9 and above. When they are not used, and the agency does not maintain its own inventories, individual vacancies are publicized directly by the hiring office or an OPM area office. For information about these opportunities, contact the Federal Job Information Center in the area where you want to work.

Federal Agencies Maintaining Separate Competitor Inventories

National Aeronautics and Space Administration (NASA): Aerospace Technologist positions GS-7/15 for all locations are recruited directly by NASA. Applicants should file with the NASA installation where they wish to work. Contact any Federal Job Information Center or NASA facility for a list of installations and addresses.

United States
Office of
Personnel
Management

DO'S

*Read carefully the vacancy announcement or the examination announcement for the position for which you are applying. Underline the skills required by the position.

*Describe *your* experience so that you emphasize the work that used the skills required by the vacant position.

*Use active verbs to describe what work *you* actually did. Be *specific.*

*Keep your experience descriptions brief.

*Write everything on the 171 itself—cut and splice a 171 with continuation forms if necessary. Eliminate blank lines.

*Use *your own words* in filling out the experience blanks.

*Include *all* experience, whether paid or volunteer.

*Arrange your experience in chronological order.

*Choose references who can remember you, and know how you perform in a work (paid or unpaid) situation.

*Have your 171 neatly and accurately typed or write so that each word is legible.

*If your 171 is reproduced, be sure every page is easily readable. Make certain the pages are in the correct order.

DONT'S

*Don't use the same 171 for jobs in non-related fields.

*Don't exaggerate.
*Don't be humble.

*Don't describe the work of the organization generally or the work of others.

*Don't use attachments. (Take them to the interview.)

*Don't *ever* use position descriptions.

*Don't omit church, community, or club work.

*Don't use general character references—they usually won't commit themselves on such matters as dependability, initiative, etc.

*Don't submit a 171 that is messy, hard to read, or confusing to follow.

*Don't make your 171 a "challenge" to the reader. Hard-to-read applications go in the "Out" pile first.

Prepared by: Carol A. Watkins for Federally Employed Women, Inc., Washington, D.C.

Physical Sciences

Employment Prospects

Occupational Specialty	Grade Group	Alaska	Atlanta	Boston	Caribbean	Chicago	Dallas	Denver	New York	Pacific	Philadelphia	St. Louis	San Francisco	Seattle	Washington D.C.
Astronomer	5/7	D				D				C		D			D
	9/11	D				D				D		D			D
	12/13	D				D				D		D			D
	14/15	D				D				D		D			D
Cartographer (See Note 1)	5/7					C	C			C	D	D			A
	9/11					D	D			D	D	D	D		C
	12/13					D	D			D	D	D	D		C
	14/15					D	D			D					D
Chemist	5/7	D			C	A	A	D	C	A	C	C*	C		B
	9/11	C			D	A	B	D	C	C	C	C*	C		B
	12/13	C			D	B	B	D	C	C	C	C*			B
	14/15	D			D	D	B	C		D	C	C*			B
Food Technologist	5/7			C						C	D	D			D
	9/11					D	D			D	D	D			D
	12/13					D	D			D	D	D			D
	14/15						D			D	D	D			D
Forest Products Technologist	5/7					D	D			C		D			D
	9/11					D	D			D		D			D
	12/13					D	D			D		D			D
	14/15					D	D			D		D			D
General Physical Scientist (See Note 1)	5/7	D			D	C	C			C	D	D	D		B
	9/11	D		D*	D	C	C			D	D	D	D		C
	12/13	D		D*	D	C	C			D	D	D	D		C
	14/15	D				D	D			D	D	D	D		C
Geodesist (See Note 1)	5/7					D	B			C	D	D	D		D
	9/11					D	D			D	D	D	D		D
	12/13					D	D			D	D	D	D		D
	14/15					D	D			D	D	D			D
Geologist	5/7	D		D	D	B	C	D		C	C	D	C		B
	9/11	D		D	D	B	B	D	C	D	C	D	C		C
	12/13	D		D	D	B	B	D		D	C	D	B		C
	14/15	D		D		B	B	C	D	C	C	D			C
Geophysicist	5/7		C*			C	B			C		D			D
	9/11	C	D*			C	C			D		D	C		D
	12/13	C	D			C	C			D		D	C		D
	14/15	C	D			D	C			D		D			D

Opportunity Codes (Subject to Change)

A. Excellent— Most qualified applicants receive job offers.
B. Good— Most well-qualified applicants receive job offers.
C. Fair— Some well-qualified applicants receive job offers.
D. Poor— Only a few of the best qualified applicants receive job offers.
No entry—(Limited). For specialties at grades GS-5/7, applications are not being accepted (unanticipated recruitment needs will be publicized locally). For specialties at grades GS-9 and above, the acceptance of applications, if needed, will be publicized through local publicity.

*Agencies/establishments may make immediate offers of employment for certain duty locations. Contact the area office in the zone for information.

Where to Apply

File your application with the area office which serves your selected zone (see below).

Zones/OPM Area Office Addresses

Alaska
Anchorage Area Office
Federal Bldg. & U.S. Courthouse
701 "C" Street, Box 22
Anchorage, Alaska 99513

Atlanta
Huntsville Area Office
Southerland Building
806 Governors Drive, S.W.
Huntsville, Alabama 35801

Boston
Boston Area Office
3 Center Plaza
Boston, Massachusetts 02108

Caribbean
Newark Area Office
970 Broad Street
Newark, New Jersey 07102

Chicago
Dayton Area Office
200 W. 2nd Street, Room 507
Dayton, Ohio 45402

Dallas
Oklahoma City Area Office
200 N.W. 5th Street, Room 205
Oklahoma City, Oklahoma 73102

Denver
Denver Area Office
1845 Sherman Street
Denver, Colorado 80203

New York
Newark Area Office
970 Broad Street
Newark, New Jersey 07102

Pacific
Honolulu Area Office
300 Ala Moana Blvd.,
P.O. Box 50028
Honolulu, Hawaii 96850

Philadelphia
Philadelphia Area Office
600 Arch Street
Philadelphia, Pennsylvania 19106

San Francisco
Los Angeles Area Office
845 S. Figueroa. 3rd Fl.
Los Angeles, California 90017

Seattle
Seattle Area Office
915 2nd Avenue, Room 2563
Seattle, Washington. 98174

St. Louis
St. Louis Area Office
1520 Market Street
St. Louis, Missouri 63103

Washington, D.C.
Washington Area Office
1900 E Street, N.W.
Washington, D.C. 20415

¹ Defense Mapping Agency (DMA) accepts applications directly for General Physical Scientists (GS-9/15), Geodesists (GS-5/15), and Cartographers (GS-5/15) at two locations: For employment at DMA locations east of the Mississippi River and overseas—DMA Hydrographic/Topographic Center, Examining and External Recruitment Center, Washington, D.C. 20315. For locations west of the Mississippi River—DMA Aerospace Center, Staffing Division, Personnel Office, 2nd and Arsenal Streets, St. Louis Air Force Station, Missouri 63118.

Employment Prospects

Specialty (Continued)	Grade Group	Alaska	Atlanta	Boston	Caribbean	Chicago	Dallas	Denver	New York	Pacific	Philadelphia	St. Louis	San Francisco	Seattle	Washington D.C.
Health Physicist	5/7		C	C	D	D	D		D	B	C	D	D	A	C
	9/11		C		D	D	D		D	B	D	A	D	A	B
	12/13		B		D	D	D		D	B	D	B	D	A	B
	14/15		D		D	D	D		D		D		D	A	C
Hydrologist	5/7		D			D	B	B			C	C	D	C	C
	9/11		D	D*		D	B	B			D	C	D	C	C
	12/13		D	D*		D	C	B			D	C	D	C	C
	14/15		D			D	D	C			D		D		C
Land Surveyor	5/7		D			D	D	B			C	D	D	B	D
	9/11		D			D	D	C			D	D	D	B	D
	12/13		D			D	D	C			D	D	D	B	D
	14/15		D			D	D	D			D		D		D
Metallurgist	5/7		D	B		B	A	B*	B	A	C	C	C*	A	A
	9/11		D	B		B	B	B*	A	A·	D	A	C*	A	B
	12/13		D	B		C	C	B	C	A	D	A	C*	A	B
	14/15		D			D	D	D	D		D		D		C
Meteorologist	5/7		D			D	B	C	D		B	D	D	C	B
	9/11	D	D			D	C	C	D	D	D	D	D	C	C
	12/13	D	C			D	C	C	D	D	D	C	D	C	C
	14/15		D			D	D	C	D		D		D		D
Oceanographer	5/7		C*			C		D			A	D	D	C	C
	9/11		C*			C		D			D	D	D	C	C
	12/13		C			C		D			D	D	D	B	C
	14/15		D			D		D			D	D	D		C
Photographic Technologist	5/7			B		D	D				C	D	D		D
	9/11					D	D				D	D	D		D
	12/13					D	D				D	D	D		D
	14/15					D	D				D	D	D		D
Physicist	5/7		B*		B*	D	B	A			A	D	C*	A	A
	9/11		B*		B*	D	C	B			C	D	C*	A	B
	12/13		B*		C	D	C	C			C	D	C*	A	B
	14/15		D			D	D	D			D		D		C
Textile Technologist	5/7			B		D		D			C		D		D
	9/11					D		D			D		D		D
	12/13					D		D			D		D		D
	14/15					D		D			D		D		D

Entrance Salaries:

GS-5	$12,854
GS-7	15,922
GS-9	19,477
GS-11	23,566
GS-12	28,245
GS-13	33,586
GS-14	39,689
GS-15	46,685

Metallurgist (these rates apply only in U.S.A.)

GS-5	$16,706
GS-7	20,701
GS-9	23,371
GS-11	25,924

U.S. GOVERNMENT PRINTING OFFICE: 1982-361-390:112

Employment Prospects

Occupational Specialty	Grade Group	Alaska	Atlanta	Boston	Caribbean	Chicago	Dallas	Denver	New York	Pacific	Philadelphia	St. Louis	San Francisco	Seattle	Washington, D.C.
Aerospace	5/7*		D*	D	D	A	B	D	A		B	A	A	A	C
	9/11*		D*	B	D	A	B	D	C		B	A	B	A	C
	12/13		C*	B*	D	B*	B	D*	D		C	B*	C*	B	D
	14/15		D		D		D	D	D		D	B	D		
Agriculture	5/7*			D		B		D	D	D					
	9/11*		D		D	D	B	D	D	D	C	B	B	A	
	12/13		D		D	D	B	D	D	D*	D	C	B	B	C
	14/15		D		D		D	D	D	D	D		D	D	C
Biomedical	5/7*	D	D	B	D	C	C	B	D		C	C	B	C	C
	9/11*	D	D	B	D	B	C	B	D		D	A	C	C	C
	12/13	D	D	B*	D	C	D	C	D		D	C	C	D	C
	14/15	D	D	D		D	D	D	D			D			C
Ceramics	5/7*		D	C	D		D		D		C		B	D	C
	9/11*		D	C	D		D		D		D		D	D	D
	12/13		D	C*	D		D		D		D		D	D	D
	14/15		D		D		D		D		D		D	D	D
Chemical	5/7*		D	D	D	A	C	C	A	C	B	D	A	A	A
	9/11*		D	D	D	B	C	C	C	C	B	D	C	A	A
	12/13		D*		D	C*	C	C*	D	C*	C	D	C	B	A
	14/15		D		D		D	D	D	D		D	C	B	B
Civil	5/7*	B	C	C	C	C	A	A	B	B	A	C	A	B	A
	9/11*	B	C	C	C	C	A	A	A	B	B	C	B	B	A
	12/13	B	D*	D	D	C	B	A*	C	B*	C	C*	C	B	A
	14/15	C	D		D		D	D	D	D	D		D	C	B
Electrical	5/7*	B	A	A	D	A	A	A	A	A	B	A	A	A	A
	9/11*	B	A	B	D	A	A	A	A	A	B	A	B	A	A
	12/13	B	A*	C*	D	B	A	A*	B	A*	B	B*	B*	A	A
	14/15		D					C	D	D	D		C	B	C
Electronic	5/7*		A	A	D	A	A	B	A	A	B	A	A	A	A
	9/11*		A	B	D	A	A	A	A	B	A	B	A	A	A
	12/13		A*	B*	D	B*	A	A*	A	B*	C	A*	B*	A	A
	14/15		D					C	D	D	D		C	B	C
Environmental	5/7*	C	D	D	D	C	B	B	B	B	B	D	A	C	C
	9/11*	C	C	D	D	C	B	B	C	B	C	D	B	C	C
	12/13	C	D*		D	D	B	B*	D	B*	D	C	C	C	D
	14/15		D		D		D	B	D	D	D		C	D	D
Fire Prevention	5/7*		D		D	D	D	D	D	D	C		B	D	C
	9/11*		D		D	D	D	D	D	D	C		C	C	B
	12/13		D*		D	D	D	C	D	D*	D		C	D	B
	14/15		D		D		D	D	D	D	D		D	D	D

Engineers

Where to Apply*

File your application with the area office which serves your selected zone (see below).

Alaska
Anchorage Area Office
Federal Bldg. & U.S. Courthouse
701 "C" Street, Box 22
Anchorage, Alaska 99513

Atlanta
Huntsville Area Office
Southerland Building
806 Governors Drive, S.W.
Huntsville, Alabama 35801

Boston
Boston Area Office
3 Center Plaza
Boston, Massachusetts 02108

Caribbean
Newark Area Office
970 Broad Street
Newark, New Jersey 07102

Chicago
Dayton Area Office
200 W. 2nd Street, Room 507
Dayton, Ohio 45402

Dallas
Oklahoma City Area Office
200 N.W. 5th Street, Room 205
Oklahoma City, Oklahoma 73102

Denver
Denver Area Office
1845 Sherman Street
Denver, Colorado 80203

New York
Newark Area Office
970 Broad Street
Newark, New Jersey 07102

Pacific
Honolulu Area Office
300 Ala Moana Blvd.,
P.O. Box 50028
Honolulu, Hawaii 96850

Philadelphia
Philadelphia Area Office
600 Arch Street
Philadelphia, Pennsylvania 191

San Francisco
Los Angeles Area Office
845 S. Figueroa, 3rd Fl.
Los Angeles, California 90017

Seattle
Seattle Area Office
915 2nd Avenue, Room 2563
Seattle, Washington 98174

St. Louis
St. Louis Area Office
1520 Market Street
St. Louis, Missouri 63103

Washington, D.C.
Washington Area Office
1900 E Street, N.W.
Washington, D.C. 20415

Opportunity Codes (Subject to Change)

A. Excellent— Most qualified applicants receive job offers.
B. Good— Most well-qualified applicants receive job offers.
C. Fair— Some well-qualified applicants receive job offers.
D. Poor— Only a few of the best qualified applicants receive job offers.
No entry—(Limited). For specialties at grades GS-5/7, applications are not being accepted (unanticipated recruitment needs will be published locally). For specialties at grades GS-9 and above, the acceptance of applications, if needed, will be publicized through local publicity.

*Federal agencies may make immediate offers of employment for their engineering positions at grades GS-5 through GS-11. This authority has been extended for higher grades for some specialties and locations as indicated by an asterisk (*) next to the opportunity code. You may apply to the agency/location where you wish to work.

Employment Prospects

Specialty (Continued)	Grade Group	Alaska	Atlanta	Boston	Caribbean	Chicago	Dallas	Denver	New York	Pacific	Philadelphia	St. Louis	San Francisco	Seattle	Washington, D.C.
Industrial	5/7*	D	B	B	D	A	B	C	A	A	B	A	A	A	C
	9/11*	D	C	B	D	A	A	C	C	A	B	A	B	A	B
	12/13	D	C*	B*	D		B*	B	C*	C	A*	C	B*		B
	14/15		D		D			C		D	D		D		B
Materials	5/7*		D	C	D	C	C	D	B			C	D	A	A
	9/11*		D	C	D	B	C	D	C			C	D	C	A
	12/13		D*	C*	D	B*	C	D	D			C	D	C	B
	14/15		D		D			D	D			D	D	D	D
Mechanical	5/7*	B	A	A	D	A	A	B	A	A	B	A	A	A	A
	9/11*	B	A	B	D	A	A	B	A	A	B	A	B	A	A
	12/13	B	A*	B*	D		B*	A	B*	B	A*	C	C*	C	A
	14/15	C	D		D			D	D	D	D		C	D	B
Mining	5/7*	B	D			D	A	C	A	D		C	D	A	D
	9/11*	B	D			D	B	C	A	D		C	D	A	C
	12/13	B	D			D	C	B	D	D		D	D	A	C
	14/15	C	D				C		D				D	B	C
Naval Architect	5/7*		D	B	D	D	D		D	A	C	D	A	B	C
	9/11*		D	C	D	D	D		D	A	C	D	B	B	A
	12/13		D	C*	D	D	D		D	B*	D	D	C	C	A
	14/15		D		D	D	D		D	D	D	D			A
Nuclear	5/7*		C	B	D	C	D		C	A	B		A	A	B
	9/11*		C	D	D	C	D		C	A	C		A	A	B
	12/13		A*	D	D	D	D		D	A*	D		A	A	B
	14/15		D						D	D	D		A	A	C
Ocean	5/7*		D	D	D	D	D		D	D	B		B	D	B
	9/11*		D	D	D	D	D		D	D	D		D	D	C
	12/13		D		D	D	D		D	D*	D		D	D	C
	14/15		D		D	D			D	D	D		D		D
Petroleum	5/7*	A	D	B	D	D	A	A	D		B	D	A	D	C
	9/11*	A	D	B	D	D	A	A	D		C	D	C	D	B
	12/13	A	D		D	D	A	B	D		D	D	C	D	B
	14/15	A	D		D		C	D	D		D		C		C
Safety	5/7*		D	D	D	C	C	D	C	C	D	A	C	C	C
	9/11*		D	C	D	C	C	D	C	D	C	D	C	C	B
	12/13		C*	D	D	D	C	D*	D	D*	D	D	D	C	B
	14/15		D				D		D		D		C		C
Welding	5/7*		D	B	D	A	D		D	A	B		A	D	C
	9/11*		D	B	D	A	D		D	A	B		C	D	D
	12/13		D	B*	D	B	D		D	B*	D		D	D	D
	14/15		D		D				D		D		D		D

Special Minimum Salary Rates

Specialties:	Petroleum	Mining	All Other
GS-5	$16,706	$16,706	$16,706
GS-7	20,701	20,701	20,701
GS-9	25,318	25,318	24,020
GS-11	30,640	29,068	25,924
GS-12	34,839	32,955	28,245
GS-13	39,186	35,826	33,586
GS-14	42,335	39,689	39,689
GS-15	46,685	46,685	46,685

Understanding
the System

While the primary focus of this chapter is on women in federal civil service, women in private employment may gain some insights into the conditions that inhibit or advance their progress as well.

On getting your first job, in federal government or in private employment, bear in mind that no one "promised you a rose garden." Once on the payroll, your future will depend in large measure on your own initiative, energy, knowledge, drive, and perseverance. But that's only part of it. How you interact with your peers and supervisors and others in a position to affect your career is equally important. Don't expect favors. Don't expect your boss to come to you and tell you how great you are and that he or she is going to promote you. It doesn't work that way.

The Civil Rights Act of 1964, the Equal Employment Opportunities Act of 1972, the Age Discrimination in Employment Act of 1967, as amended in 1974 and 1978, and a multiplicity of executive orders issued over the years by presidents of the United States were intended to eliminate employment discrimination based on race, creed, color, national origin, age, and sex. But the ugly fact remains that sex discrimination is subtle and pervasive and continues as a major factor in the failure of women to achieve their highest potential.

A number of studies by psychologists and sociologists have proclaimed that women don't get ahead because they fear success. Other studies contend women fear failure and therefore do not strive for success. Maybe there is some truth to these allegations. But based on my experiences, dealing with thousands of men and women over many years, I cannot accept such hypotheses without a challenge. I have worked with men who had the same fears and never advanced in their careers. Fear is not an exclusive female characteristic.

Today's woman who is prepared to enter the work force with a solid educational background and confidence in her abilities, with clearly defined goals and objectives and loads of ambition stands a better chance to overcome sex discrimination if she is astute, subtle, wise in the ways of human behavior, determined to succeed, and prepared to take risks.

Of course it is not all that simple. True, there are no signs posted along the way that proclaim "men only" at the entrance to management or senior-level professional jobs, but they are there nonetheless, written in invisible ink. One has but to look at the statistics on women's employment in high-salaried positions for the evidence. It's dismal.

In 1978, the Bureau of the Census reported that 5.6 percent of full-time working men earned more than $25,000 in managerial jobs, while women in comparable jobs made up only .4 percent of full-time working women.

A 1980 survey of the country's top fifty industrial companies, conducted by Spencer Stuart and Associates, a New York Executive Search firm, found only 400 (fewer than 5 percent) of managers earning $40,000 or more were women.

More women are entering professional and technical fields than ever before. Data collected by the Bureau of Labor Statistics, U.S. Department of Labor, shows that among a selected group of occupations in professional and technical areas, 43.3 percent of more than 15 million jobs were held by women. This represents an increase of 23.8 percent between 1975 and 1979.

Significant among these changes is the percentage of women in areas previously regarded as male preserves: accountants—32.9 percent women in 1979, compared with 23.7 percent in 1974; lawyers and judges—12.4 percent women in 1979, but only 7 percent in 1974.

It is clearly evident in federal government that women in the professions, as well as in nonprofessional jobs, are subject to covert employment discrimination.

For example, a study conducted over the past two years in the Geologic Division of the U.S. Geological Survey ". . . found that women, as a group, have been hired at lower grades than men having the same college degree; that promotion rates have commonly been slower for women than for men; that a smaller percentage of women than men were promoted by means of selection to administrative and management positions; that median and mean grades of women in 1978 were one to two GS grades lower than those of men having comparable education; and that a significant salary disparity between men and women existed. The disparity was $4,400 for women hired before 1970 and $3,400 for women hired from 1970 to 1978."

While the narrowing of the salary gap may be interpreted as "progress," the fact remains, women are not treated equally in the world of work. Similar disparities exist throughout the federal service and in the private sector. Court dockets are loaded with cases alleging salary discrimination based on sex. Many such cases have been won, with back pay awards running into millions of dollars.

Nationwide, as of March 1979, among employed persons between the ages of twenty-five and sixty-four, with four years of college, men held 28.7 percent of manager and administrator positions, while women held 9.7 percent of these occupations.

In federal service women held only 5.8 percent of top jobs as of September 1980. There certainly is no lack of qualified women to fill these billets.

Considering that the laws and executive orders mandating equality of opportunity have been in effect since the mid-1960s, one would hope the decade of the 1980s holds more promising opportunities for women. But social customs, attitudes, and traditions are not readily changed. Discrimination against working women is not a twentieth century phenomenon. Let's look at a bit of history.

Discrimination against women in public service antedates the Constitution itself. In 1773, when a woman was appointed Postmaster in Baltimore, she faced rather formidable opposition from no less a person than Thomas Jefferson, who said: "The appointment of a woman to office is an innovation for which the public is not prepared."

Though few would voice such sentiments today, the attitude underlying the statement still prevails.

A little more than a century ago, June 11, 1870, to be exact, Representative Willard of Vermont participated in a debate in the House of Representatives on legislation that was to influence the employment of women in the federal government for the next ninety-two years. The debate concerned an appropriation bill with a rider that would require equal pay for equal work irrespective of sex.

In his argument for it, Representative Willard said: "I hold that this government owes it to the women of the country ... that they shall no longer be held in a subordinate position and treated as inferiors; that it shall say to them there shall be hereafter no position under this government for which they are fitted which shall not be open to them equally with men; that when they do work of any of their brothers in any office under the government, they shall have the same pay their brothers have; that their brains are worth as much, that their labor, their energy, their industry are all worth as much as the labor, the industry, the energy, and the brains of anybody. If the women of the country had the ballot today—as I believe they ought to have it—then this House would be found voting unanimously for this proposition ... "

In the final analysis, the provision was watered down to *permit* appointing officers to employ "female clerks" at the same pay as men.

Ironically, although this 1870 statute was intended to benefit women in the matter of pay, it was construed by appointing officers as giving them unrestricted right to selective hiring on the basis of sex.

In its annual report to Congress for the year ending June 30, 1891, the Civil Service Commission reported 147 women appointed from competitive examinations to the departmental service and 776 men. The ratio of women to men was a little less than one to five.

The following year, June 30, 1892, the Commission's report stated the number of women appointed was 86 and the number of men 245, the proportion being a little more than one to three.

By way of explanation, the report stated: "It is difficult to account for this change, but attention is called to the fact as one of general interest and as probably showing that the prejudice which has heretofore existed to some extent against the appointment of women in the classified service is gradually disappearing."

This same report, commenting on an increase in promotions of women, stated: "These promotions have been won on the basis of the efficiency records kept in the departments and the close competitive tests which have supplemented those records and show that when women in the public service have a fair and even chance with the men, they win their full share of the more lucrative and responsible positions."

So here we are, ninety years later, "protected" by statutes against employment discrimination based on sex, and we find that women in public service do not get a "fair and even chance with men," nor have they begun to win even a modest share of the more "lucrative and responsible positions."

But, "hope springs eternal . . ." Between 1968 and 1971, headlines were made when a few women were appointed to positions in occupations normally regarded as the male preserve. For example, one woman was appointed a tug boat captain; other appointments included a customs inspector; aviation operations inspector; and a gyro repair foreman. Of course these so-called "breakthroughs" were pure tokenism. The nation did not collapse because a few women were doing "men's work."

Admittedly, the number of women who might seek employment in fields such as these is comparatively small. But that is not the issue. The basic issue is that all qualified persons, regardless of sex, race, color, and everything else, are entitled to choose the occupation they want by reason of education, training, skill, motivation, physical stamina, personal desire, and ambition.

In November, 1969, the Civil Service Commission issued a report entitled "Characteristics of the Federal Executive." It included all employees in grades GS-15 and above. Of the 28,000 employees occupying positions at these levels, 584, or 2 percent, were women. More than one-third of the women were medical officers; one in six was a social scientist; and less than 1 percent of the top executives in supply management, logistics, fiscal occupations (including accounting), business occupations (including contracting), engineering, and physical sciences were women.

How to explain this unconscionably poor showing? Certainly there was no shortage of qualified women. Rather the problem stems from long-standing social customs, traditions, life patterns, and the male perception of women's role in society—perpetuation of stereotypes.

In 1970, the President's Task Force on Women's Rights and Responsibilities issued a report of its comprehensive study on women, entitled "A Matter of Simple Justice." One paragraph tells it all:

> Social attitudes are slow to change. So widespread and prevasive are discrimination practices against women that they have come to be regarded, more often than not, as *normal*. Unless there is a clear indication of administration concern at the highest level, it is unlikely that significant progress can be made in correcting ancient, entrenched injustices.

Needless to say, there was no stampede to provide "clear indication of administration concern at the highest level," but there began a gradual awakening of the need to recognize the potential of women.

The gate swung open slightly during the Nixon administration, wider during the Ford administration, and still wider during the Carter years. In fact, women's greatest gains in public service were made between 1976 and 1980.

In each of these administrations a woman was appointed to the White House staff to oversee the recruitment of women for high-level positions. But, as the saying goes, "You can lead a horse to water, but you can't make him drink." Convincing the bureaucrats, the heads of agencies, of the need to be responsive to the White House dictum to employ more women, was another story. Men seem to tense their mental muscles in resisting change.

In the late 1960s and early 1970s, as educated women became increasingly aware and restive about their second-class status, they began to organize for a common purpose—equal opportunity in the marketplace—in government, business, and academe.

Federally Employed Women (FEW), born in 1968, has been a continuing force in gaining recognition for women in federal service. The National Women's Political Caucus has labored diligently in the political arena to increase the number of women in elective office. The Women's Equity Action League (WEAL) has many stars in its crown for its achievements in battling discrimination, particularly in institutions of higher learning. The National Association of Women Business Owners (NAWBO) has coalesced around the issue of sharing the wealth—getting government contracts for women-owned businesses. The largest and strongest group in the struggle for equal rights and equal justice for women is the National Organization for Women (NOW).

Literally, hundreds of women's organizations, some old, mostly new, have been making their voices heard. Many concentrate on improving the economic status of women in a particular discipline: Women in Science, Society of Women Engineers, Nuclear Energy Women, Women in Communications, Sociologists for Women in Society, to name just a very few. Others are single-issue oriented: ERAmerica, National Association for Girls and Women in Sports, Association for Women in Psychology, Washington Women Economists. Within many national professional organizations women members have organized committees and caucuses to gain recognition for their achievements and their potential for contributing still more to meet the societal, cultural, and educational needs of our nation.

Shortly after Jimmy Carter was elected President of the United States, a group of women, under the auspices of the National Women's Political Caucus, organized the Coalition for Women's Appointments. Representatives of hundreds of women's organizations participated in the work of the Coalition, whose goal was to ensure that women got a reasonable share of the high-level appointive government positions.

No politician can afford to ignore the Coalition. It represents hundreds of thousands of enlightened women who view the ballot box as a bridge to power.

In due course, the Carter administration appointed the largest number of women to high public office in the history of the United States. Though it was an historical "first," it fell far short of the goals anticipated and projected by women's organizations. The saving grace was that these women appointees in turn appointed and promoted women, many already in the career service, whose talents had long been underutilized for no other reason than that they were women.

In 1981, the scene changed. When the nation's leadership changes, particularly to a different political party, so do the faces. Presidential and political appointees are the most vulnerable people in government. Those who labor in the vineyards for the election of political candidates expect to be rewarded with top jobs in government. That's the name of the game. Men and women appointed during the Carter administration are gone. Thirty-three percent of senior government officers during his administration were women. Today the number has been considerably reduced.

Although President Reagan purported to support equal employment opportunity for women, he disavowed the Republican Party's long-standing support for the Equal Rights Amendment. He appointed to high office only men who shared his ultraconservative views. In turn, these men appointed other men of like mind to run the government. Witness the statistics. As of January, 1982, only one of eighteen cabinet-level positions was held by a woman, the United States Ambassador to the United Nations. Of approximately 400 positions requiring Senate approval, only forty-three were filled by women.

By March 1983 the number had increased to 45.

After the November 1982 Congressional election, the Administration was stunned by the number of seats lost in the House of Representatives to pro-feminist legislators. The White House invited the Chair of the National Women's Political Caucus to meet with a few of the President's advisors to find out how they could overcome the perception among women that the nation was being run like a men's club. Her advice to them was to stop running the country like a men's club and promote women into top positions.

Shortly thereafter the Secretary of Transportation and the Secretary of Health and Human Services resigned. The President appointed two women to fill these cabinet-level positions. Elizabeth Dole, wife of Senator Robert Dole, who had been on the White House staff in charge of public liaison, was named Secretary of Transportation. Congresswoman Margaret Heckler, who lost her campaign for reelection to the House of Representatives, was appointed Secretary of Health and Human Services.

Had these two vacancies occurred before the Congressional election, chances are the positions would have been filled by men. As evidence, witness the fact that when the Secretary of State, Secretary of Energy, and the National Security Advisor resigned some months earlier, they were replaced by other men. Male candidates have been nominated for two more existing vacancies (heads of the Environmental Protection Agency and the Arms Control and Disarmament Agency).

In practice, this administration appears to support the concept that woman is "... cricket on the hearth and man is eagle on the wing." They are happiest when she chirps away in domestic tranquility rather than compete in "a man's world."

These are not the best of times for women in federal government.

Furthermore, Congress approved the President's budget for 1982, which called for an enormous buildup of our military might. To accomplish this objective, all government agencies, except the Department of Defense, suffered substantial reductions in their budgets. Budget cuts mean elimination or reduction of many programs, and substantial reductions in the workforce. It is anticipated that 100,000 fewer federal employees will be on the payroll by 1985.

Reductions in force occur in several ways: not filling vacant positions; not replacing employees who resign, retire, or die; abolishing jobs by eliminating programs and projects and the people who carry them out; and by closing field offices across the nation.

Although the Office of Personnel Management set up a task force for the purpose of helping employees being fired through no fault of their own, to be placed in agencies that do have authorized positions to fill, the program has been largely ignored.

Despite this gloomy picture, I urge you not to give up hope. Each administration asserts its power in different ways, and under our system of government, they come and go every few years. I served under six presidents in the course of my government career and watched each of their administrations come in with a bunch of new brooms determined to sweep out the agencies and remold them in their own images. Massive reorganizations took place. People were shuffled around like a game of checkers. But the majority of civil servants continued to perform their respective duties, albeit sometimes in a different environment, with some changes in focus or direction, but essentially with little impact on their overall performance.

The Reagan administration, taking advantage of the loopholes created by the Carter administration's Civil Service Reform Act, effectively decimated the ranks of senior level, career civil servants. But like their predecessors, this group will pass on, and in due course the government will expand to meet the needs of its constituents.

So if federal employment is your goal, it may take a bit longer to get in and eventually move up, but you should keep trying.

Statisticians, health professionals, librarians, management analysts, economists, scientists, accountants, technicians, engineers, administrative officers, clerks and secretaries, and many other professionals go about their daily tasks regardless of who is in power.

Such upheavals are not unique to the federal government. They occur equally in the private sector. The appointment of a new chief executive officer, or the takeover of one company by another, often triggers massive changes in the corporation, including firing employees whose services are deemed no longer necessary.

There are no guarantees in the world of work.

So, while the prospects for appointment and career advancement for women may not seem promising at this time in our history, it is important to continue to work toward your personal career development goals and to look ahead.

For those untouched by reductions in force, now is the time to seek opportunity for promotion to existing vacancies or assignment to other jobs for which one is qualified. The business of government does go on. With fewer people to do the work, this may be the chance you have been waiting for to demonstrate your worth and potential.

On that optimistic note, how do you work your way through the "system"?

Theoretically you should start working on your career goals the first day you go to work. Admittedly, I have yet to meet the person who has done that. Most of us need to dip our toes in the water first before we get into the swim of things.

If you're wondering where to start, think in terms of planning a cross-country motor trip. You start with a road map, plot your course, plan your itinerary—how many miles you expect to cover each day, where you plan to spend the nights, and finally, when you expect to arrive at your destination.

Translating that analogy to the world of work, your first decision is where do you want to go (your road map), or you should at least have a sense of where you want to go. Then establish your priorities by setting some goals and objectives and then devoting yourself to achieving them.

It sounds very simplistic, but that's what career planning is all about. Getting ahead begins with you and your capacity, eagerness, and determination for growth and advancement.

Begin by examining the "climate" in your organization, especially toward women. Is it filled with roadblocks or are there some welcome mats lying around?

Some things to think about:

- How supportive is your supervisor? Are you being encouraged and complimented for a job well done? Are the lines of communication between you and your supervisor open?
- Do you have a good relationship with your peers? Is there a support system within the organization?
- Do you see prospects for advancement in your office or your agency as a whole?
- How far have you progressed since you started to work? How long have you been at the same grade level and in the same job?
- What incentives have you received that would motivate you toward striving for better opportunities?
- Have you looked around to see where the women are in your agency? Are there any (or many) in supervisory or management positions?
- Are there just one or two "token" women in upper levels, or is there evidence that women are moving up?

Notwithstanding the laws, rules, regulations, and policies mandating equal opportunity for women, no one gives away POWER. Women who want a "piece of the action" are going to have to work twice as hard as men to get their share. Competition is keen.

There are many mediocre men in top jobs and they are accepted. I have met and worked with lots of them. But mediocrity in women will not be tolerated. So women must prepare themselves to be the best qualified individuals for the jobs to which they aspire. At the same time it is important to learn and understand organizational dynamics. Who are the people who are advancing, and why? How do you make yourself known to those in control, who can influence your future?

In planning how to gain access to jobs that offer an opportunity to reach your maximum potential, you need to do some self-evaluation.

With pad and pencil, in a relaxed environment, ask yourself these questions and jot down your answers:

- What have I got to offer, that is, what are my skills and talents?
- What are my strengths and weaknesses?
- What are my personal values? Money? Prestige? Power? Or a chance to do meaningful work and be paid accordingly?
- Can I cope with the demands of a professional job and still enjoy a fulfilling personal life? Is it really important to me that I be able to do both?
- What firm career decisions have I made? Are they attainable?
- How do I go about achieving my goals?

Questions such as these are just the beginning of your self-analysis.

- Have you approached your supervisor recently about opportunities for career development that could lead to advancement?
- Have you talked with the training officer in your agency to ascertain what training opportunities are open to you that could help make you a more effective employee and a greater asset to the organization?
- Do you have an up-to-date resume on hand in case a position to which you aspire becomes available?

Dozens of people have told me how they missed out on an opportunity to apply for a position because they only learned of the vacancy on the closing date for receipt of applications and had no resume on hand nor the time to prepare one by the deadline.

Now make a list of the "support" people in your life. One or more individuals you can rely on for advice and counsel or friendly admonishment from time to time. Jot down their names, relationship to you (boss, parent, spouse, friend, mentor, peer), and the role they play in your life (counselor, mentor, role model, critic, admirer, and so on).

What emerges from this brief analysis? Do you feel you have done a good job in planning for your future or do you feel you need to develop a more structured plan?

Are there at least five people in your support system you can count on for advice, counsel, or just a shoulder to lean on? If there are fewer than five, chances are you have been keeping too much to yourself and need to unfold and broaden your network.

Whether you think you've done a good job planning for your future so far or believe you need to develop a more structured plan, it is important to set out some specific goals for yourself.

Have you included volunteer work in listing your skills? Depending upon the nature of it and the amount of time devoted to it, volunteer work can have significant impact on your eligibility for certain higher-level jobs.

Have you ever been a Girl Scout or Campfire Girl leader, or president or vice president of a professional organization? In any of these capacities you acquired some leadership skills that could well be the deciding factor in your eligibility for a supervisory position.

Think back over your life experiences. Have you ever done a public relations job for an organization, such as recruiting new members and spreading the word about the merits of the organization? Have you ever organized or planned a conference? Managed a fundraising function? Written or edited a newsletter, maybe in high school or college? Have you ever given a speech? Do you regard yourself as a good speaker, one with the ability to hold the attention of an audience so they don't doze off during your presentation? These are valuable communications skills, critical factors in management and supervisory positions.

As you compile your list of strengths, start with "I." I'm a good speaker; I write well; I'm a good organizer; I manage money well; I'm a good researcher; I have an excellent memory (great for a job as a librarian or actress); I'm a good mixer—I can get a group of people involved in discussion; I make friends easily and keep them; I like to do things to help other people without expecting something in return (a virtue not everyone can claim); I'm a good manager—I manage children/husband/home/job and still find time for personal pursuits. Surely you can add to this list. Don't be modest about them. If you don't have faith in your own talents, you can hardly expect an employer to consider them meritorious.

After you have made a list and are satisfied that you have done a thorough job, rearrange the items in the order of YOUR MAJOR STRENGTHS. Take the top five. Are you using these skills in your present job? If not, why not? Often the failure to use the talents you have leads to frustration, disillusionment, and lack of enthusiasm for your work. When this occurs, your motivation is gone and you are not likely to be a candidate for promotion. On the other hand, your boss may not be aware of your skills, particularly the underutilized ones. Consider sitting down with him or her, with the list of your major strengths, and discuss the prospects for making a greater contribution to the organization.

Before you do that, make another list of those aspects of your present job that you *like*: opportunity to use your education and training; supportive boss; challenging work; opportunity to exercise independent judgment in accomplishing assignments; good office morale; supportive coworkers, and so on. Then rank these items in order of their importance to you.

Make another list of those aspects of your job you *dislike*: underpaid for doing same level and kind of work as male peers; too many deadlines; lack of communication with supervisor; unfriendly atmosphere; no prospects for advancement, and so on.

Are you in a position to control changes in the conditions of work? List those you, your supervisor, or your peers could change to make for a better work environment that would help you become more productive.

Make a similar list for things that cannot be changed, either by you, your supervisor, or your peers.

If the things that you don't like about your job and the things that cannot be changed outnumber the satisfactions, maybe you had better start looking elsewhere. Not necessarily in another organization but possibly within your present one.

Now that you have examined your skills and strengths and your satisfactions (or dissatisfactions) with your present job, it is time to focus on where you plan to be, professionally, in the next two years. What grade or job title are you aiming for and determined to acquire? Make a similar plan for five years hence.

Having set some realistic targets for yourself, the next question is: Do you have all the skills and knowledge necessary for the job to which you aspire?

Before you can answer that accurately, you need to know what skills and knowledges and/or training or experience are essential for the job(s) you have in mind. If you find you lack some of the requirements, your next step is to set about acquiring the necessary "tools."

In federal civil service, *Handbook X-118* lists the qualification standards (requirements) for every classified position in the system. It is the working "bible" of every personnel specialist engaged in recruiting and evaluating candidates for appointments and promotions. Copies are available in every federal personnel office and in agency libraries. You are entitled to consult them. But bear in mind that these are only the minimum qualification requirements. Civil service examination announcements contain the same information plus specific additional details that will be used in determining your eligibility for a particular occupation. Samples of the *Handbook X-118* qualification standards for the Management Analysis Series appear at the end of this chapter.

Agencies are required to post vacancy announcements on all bulletin boards. As a rule, these are listed as Merit Program Vacancy Announcements. If one appears in your specialty, study it carefully to ascertain what specific qualifications may be required. If you find you need additional specialized training or education to become eligible, it's time to see your agency training officer or your supervisor. Find out what training programs are available that would enable you to get the specialized training required for the job. Don't keep the fact that you are seeking advancement opportunities a secret. It is to your credit to be ambitious.

Consider taking additional courses, if needed, at your own expense. Many local colleges, particularly in Washington, D.C., offer courses tailored to the needs of public administration.

Talk with your supervisor about the prospects for a "detail" (temporary reassignment) for a few months to the unit or section where the work you want to do is being performed. That's one of the best ways to begin to move into another area and to find out if the job you think you want really is for you. It is also an opportunity to become known to the people who do the hiring. The key is to convince management that your goals are not solely for personal gratification, but rather that it would be in the best interests of the agency to utilize your potential to the fullest.

Another clue to successful advancement is a thorough knowledge of the agency for which you work, not just what your particular section does. What is the overall mission of the organization? Who is who in the management hierarchy? Information is POWER. Being well-informed about an entire activity can open many doors.

Read the agency's Annual Report to Congress. While not the most exciting reading matter, it provides valuable information and insights about the organization's accomplishments as well as its unfinished business. Pick up the technical language used by the professionals and use it wherever and whenever you can. With this knowledge you can more effectively plot your career path.

In addition to developing and improving your skills, knowledge, and abilities, and knowing all about the mission of your agency and who does what, keep your eyes and ears open to what's going on throughout the agency. Look around. Find out where the jobs are and what organizational changes are in the works (secretaries usually are a fountain of information).

Although posting vacancy announcements is a requirement, far too often selections are made before the official announcement. Develop a network within the organization. For example, don't lunch with the same bunch every day. Meet new people. Don't hesitate to talk "shop" with your colleagues. That doesn't mean spending time criticizing your boss or other staff members. That can be dangerous. You never know who is listening or who likes to pass along gossip. Don't gripe. If you do, the word will soon get around and people will avoid you like the plague.

"Shop talk" simply means discussing programs in which you are engaged (unless you are involved with confidential or secret activities); sharing ideas with your colleagues; exchanging views; finding out what other people do; and not hesitating to drop a hint here and there of your interest in upward mobility. You never know when it might bear fruit. By knowing of your interest in career advancement, an associate can feed you the word through the "grapevine" when a suitable vacancy occurs.

Many years ago, after lunching with a group of people, including a few computer specialists, my secretary came to me one day and asked if I would recommend her for training as a computer programmer. After twelve years as a secretary in government, she had advanced as far as possible under the job classification system for secretaries. As a single woman in her midthirties, she felt it was time for a change. She was bright, intelligent, and ambitious. I admired her for it.

Since the computer specialty was totally unrelated to her duties as a secretary, she could not qualify for training at government expense at that time. Instead, I encouraged her to take some courses at night on her own, in order to meet the basic educational requirements in the field. She did. After one year I arranged to have her detailed to a three-month stint in the computer center. Subsequently she was offered a position in the center and was on her way to a new and more satisfying career with prospects for earning considerably higher salary in due time.

About a year after getting my secretary launched on her new career, I decided it was time to take stock of my own career. After five-and-a-half years on that job I saw no prospects for further advancement and concluded it was time to look elsewhere. I succeeded in transferring to another government agency where, it turned out, I was the only professional woman in a division of 35 professional men. The clerical staff was entirely female.

The first day on my new job my boss introduced me to all the people in the division, explained my duties, and left me to fend for myself.

Realizing I needed to know more about the organization than just my small piece of the action, I went to our public information office and asked for copies of the organization chart, the annual report that goes to Congress each year, and copies of all the publications they distribute to the general public on every aspect of the agency's mission. After studying the material, I took advantage of every opportunity to ask questions of everyone I thought might know things I ought to know.

While learning a great deal about the organization as a whole, I found I knew relatively little about the people in the other branches within our division, and even less about what they were doing. It was time to find out.

My boss and his deputy and several other branch and deputy branch chiefs went to lunch together every day. I had been in the agency almost two months and never was invited to join them.

One day, as my boss reached for his coat on the way to his luncheon rendevous with "the boys," I stopped him and asked if he'd mind if I came along. He looked a little embarrassed and said, "Well, this is kind of an all-boys group, you know; you might feel a bit uncomfortable." I ignored that comment and said that my interest in going with them was to get to know my colleagues, there wasn't much opportunity during the working day because everyone was too busy. He shrugged his shoulders and said, "OK, come along if you wish." It was hardly a warm invitation. But I accepted.

When we arrived at the gathering spot in the lobby, several startled faces looked up as they saw me strolling toward them alongside my boss. One of the men asked, somewhat hesitantly, if I was joining them for lunch. I'm sure he expected me to say "no." Instead, I said, with what I hoped was a disarming smile, "Yes, is that OK with you?" Instead of responding, he looked at my boss, who replied, "It's OK, fellas, she's one of the boys."

I wanted to pounce on him for that remark, but thought that was not the appropriate moment to educate him or any of the others, for that matter. So off we went, six male chauvinists and I!

It was an enlightening experience. I learned a great deal about the organization and about them. One thing was clear—women have no monopoly on gossip!

The next day, to my surprise, my boss stopped by my office and asked if I would care to join the "gang" for lunch. I declined, with thanks, saying I had other plans but would be delighted to come the next day. I had no other plans. I wanted to give them a chance to discuss their reaction to my intruding on their male preserve.

Apparently my presence was not as discomfiting as my boss had implied when I first invited myself to their daily outing. Thereafter one of the men or my boss would poke a head in my door and say, "let's go eat." About twice a week I went with them. Obviously I had passed the test and now was a member of the "in-group."

I must confess that taking that initial step—inviting myself to lunch—was not a spur-of-the-moment decision. I had given it considerable thought for a few weeks, debating whether I should do it, whether they would think I was being "pushy," and wondering how I would react if I were turned down. Finally I decided to take the chance and risk the possibility of rejection. I convinced myself that I would survive one way or the other. I did. In the process I learned something about myself. Being assertive did not damage my reputation nor my status in the organization. My self-confidence was reinforced.

In due course I became a deputy branch chief and later chief of a new unit within the division. Having the support of my peers helped.

It is important to build an information network within your own agency. Identify the people who have real power. Build a team and a support system. Develop good internal public relations. Become alert to and aware of the ever-present office politics. Find out who is in the "in-group" and get to know some of them. Steer clear of the "out-group." There's at least one in every organization, in government as well as in private industry. Association with people who are persona non grata can do you irreparable harm.

If someone helps you get an interview for a job—whether or not you get the job—be sure to drop a note or make a telephone call to express your appreciation for the lead. Do the same with the person who interviews you. People remember these courteous gestures.

A brief word on your "image." Within the past several years a plethora of books have appeared that would lead you to believe that if you dressed like a fashion plate, you would surely be on your way to the executive suite. While I would be the first to stress that personal appearance is important, it takes more than a wardrobe to move up the career ladder. Carrying a $150 leather briefcase won't open doors for you if you lack the skills, knowledge, education, experience, ability, and motivation to prove your value to the organization. As one of my colleagues so often advises: "Dress for the boardroom, not the bedroom."

Are you on a career path to success? Probably so, if you are willing and able to take charge of your life. Intelligence, initiative, technical competence, and drive are primary paths to success. Equally important are emotional maturity and the ability to work effectively with others or alone.

Successful people possess other internal resources. They have a sense of humor and an awareness of self; they know their strengths and weaknesses and are able to balance their lives. To them life is an ongoing learning process. They are prepared to take risks and are not afraid of failure. If they fail in one endeavor, they do not let it ruin their future. Instead, they bounce back and try again, sometimes choosing a different course, but never despairing. They are sensitive to the needs of others and accept the fact that no one is perfect.

Successful people live by the philosophy so aptly described by the French philosopher Henri Bergson: "To exist is to change, to change is to mature, to mature is to go on creating oneself endlessly."

The following pages contain sample qualification standards from *Handbook X-118* Management Analysis Series. All standards in *Handbook X-118* specify the experience and education requirements for each grade level and the amount and kind of education that may be substituted for experience.

MANAGEMENT ANALYSIS SERIES[1]

All positions in grades GS-5 through GS-15

Management Analyst
Supervisory Management Analyst
Management Analysis Officer

---

[1]Cancels and supersedes the standard for this series that was issued in December 1968 and revised in October 1970.

Description of Work

Management analysts provide advice and service to management in such areas as planning; policy development; work methods and procedures; manpower utilization; organizational structures; distribution of assignments; delegation of authority; information management; or similar areas with the objective of improving managerial effectiveness. The paramount qualifications required are a high order of analytical ability and a practical and theoretical knowledge of the functions, processes, and principles of management.

Experience And Education: Table of Minimum Requirements

Grade	General experience (years)	Specialized experience (years)	Total experience (years)
GS-5	3	0	3
GS-7	3	1	4
GS-9	3	2	5
GS-11/15	3	3	6

General Experience or Education

For positions at grades GS-5 and above, applicants must have a background of one of the following:

A. A full 4-year course in an accredited college or university leading to a bachelor's degree;
B. Three years of experience in administrative, professional, investigative, technical or other responsible work which demonstrated possession of the abilities and aptitudes required to perform management analysis work;
C. Any time equivalent combination of experience and education defined in A. and B. above. In combining education with experience, an academic year of study which comprised 30 semester hours or 45 quarter hours is considered equivalent to 9 months of experience.

Specialized Experience

This is experience which has provided the opportunity to acquire and the need to apply an extensive body of practical and theoretical knowledge of the principles, functions and processes of management. In addition to management analysis experience, the following types of experience may have resulted in the development of management analysis knowledges, skills, and abilities:

A. Managing, administering, or directing an organizational segment and its work program with responsibility for planning, organizing, staffing, directing, coordinating, reporting and budgeting;

B. Analyzing and evaluating the effectiveness of management controls, channels of communication, operating procedures, organization, flow of work, etc., for example, as an internal or operational auditor;

C. Performing analytical duties in any of such occupations as budget planning, industrial engineering, production planning, program systems or operations analysis, etc., when a principal emphasis of the work was to improve management effectiveness rather than to resolve only technical problems in the field.

D. Performing job evaluation or position classification when the work included responsibility for observing and influencing management practices relating to organization of work, manpower utilization, establishment of positions, and similar matters through guiding management efforts to manage and control positions in line with sound, economical administration.

E. Performing *analytical* work in any of the areas of information management (also called records management, paperwork management, documentation management, etc.).

Note: Although this *analytical* work is now classified to this series and therefore qualifying as specialized experience, it is specifically mentioned here because it has been classified under many series codes in the past.

Substitution of Education

Full-time² graduate education may be substituted on the following basis. The education must have equipped the candidate with the knowledge and ability to perform fully the work of the position for which he is being considered.

A. *For 1 year of specialized experience*—One full academic year of graduate education in business administration, industrial management, industrial engineering, industrial psychology, public administration,

---

²Part-time graduate education is also acceptable at the rate of 30 semester hours (or the equivalent) for 1 year of specialized experience.

political science, government, or other directly related fields. (This amount and kind of education meets all the requirements for grade GS-7.)

B. *For 2 years of specialized experience*—Completion of all requirements for a master's or equivalent degree, or 2 full academic years of graduate education, which is in the fields described in paragraph A. above. (This amount and kind of education meets all the requirements for grade GS-9.)

The Superior Academic Achievement Standard in section III of part II of this handbook is applicable at grade GS-7.

Quality of Experience

All applicants, except those who qualify on the basis of education, must have had, when applying for positions at grades GS-11 and below, at least 6 months of experience at a level equivalent to the next lower grade in the Federal service, or 1 year equivalent to the second lower grade. Applicants for grades GS-12 and above must have had at least 1 year of experience equivalent to the next lower grade.

Supervisory Positions

For supervisory positions, see the qualification standard for "Supervisory Positions in General Schedule Occupations," in part III of this handbook.

Written Test

Applicants for competitive appointment to grades GS-5 and GS-7 must pass an appropriate written test. For inservice placement actions, the test is *not* required and, therefore, may *not* be used on a pass-fail basis. In addition, the test may *not* be used in evaluating or ranking eligible employees unless the test is approved for this purpose by the Civil Service Commission. (See section A-3, appendix A, FPM Supplement 335-1.)

Selective Placement

Management analysis positions vary in organizational setting, function, and operational conditions. Agencies are encouraged to use selective placement of candidates to assure an optimum match between the capabilities of candidates and the exact requirements of positions to be filled.

Basis of Rating

Applicants for grades GS-5 and GS-7 will be rated on the basis of their written test scores.

Candidates for positions at grades GS-9 and above will be rated on the basis of the quality and extent of their total experience, education, and training. Ratings will be based on statements in the application forms and any additional information received.

Personal Characteristics

Competitors must demonstrate that they possess the personal characteristics which are needed for performance of management analysis work including, for example, skill in oral expression, ability to explain and defend work products, effectiveness in personal relations, interest in management, objectivity, poise, etc. Candidates may be evaluated on these elements through the use of interviews. Applicants who do not demonstrate possession of the required characteristics to an appropriate degree will not be appointed.

Guide for Inservice Placement

In order to provide a means whereby an applicant's experience and abilities can be systematically evaluated and made a matter of record, the following evaluation procedure covering many of the characteristics which must be possessed by management analysts has been provided.

The characteristics and skills required by a management analyst vary to some degree with the nature of the specific position to be filled. Therefore, some of the characteristics and skills in the list which follows will be of greater importance in some positions than others.

Skill in oral and written expression: The ability to communicate both orally and in writing are important. This factor provides for consideration of the extent to which applicants are able to demonstrate that they can organize and develop clear and meaningful written communications such as reports and studies and can demonstrate the ability to present orally and discuss complex matters in a clear and convincing manner.

Ability to defend and sell work products: This measures the extent to which applicants can gain acceptance of their work products by their ability to work with others, ability to present ideas in the right way, the ability to persuade others, and their understanding of the need for compromise.

Creativity in solving management problems: This factor measures the degree to which applicants are able to visualize needed changes and improvements in the management process and are capable of originating new and different solutions to problems.

Effectiveness in personal relations with all levels of responsibility: This factor deals with the relative ability of the applicant to understand the roles and responsibilities of various levels of the management process and to gauge his relationships accordingly, taking into account the variety of interrelationships, motivations and goals of the members of the organization served; and his awareness of his staff role and willingness to function in such capacity.

Interest in the management process: This considers the extent to which the applicant has a deep interest in the obligations and challenges of the management process; a continually increasing comprehension and knowledge of the theoretical and practical aspects of the literature on the management process; and a desire to contribute to the advancement of such knowledge of management and the techniques and principles which underlie the process.

Analysis of complex problems: The extent to which the applicant demonstrates that he can comprehend, interrelate, evaluate facts, distinguish between causes and effects, understand fundamental problems and is able to develop solutions logically and systematically.

Practical and theoretical knowledge of management functions, theories, and techniques: This factor is used to consider the extent to which the applicant demonstrates that he has a specialized knowledge of the management process. This knowledge must be sufficiently broad and must be used with a sufficient degree of competence to permit him to resolve a management problem.

Understanding the role of management analysis in helping the organization achieve its goals: This factor is used to evaluate the degree to which the applicant understands the goals of the organization served and the means whereby these goals are reached, and possesses an appreciation of the role of management analysis in achieving these goals.

Objectivity: The degree to which the applicant demonstrates the capacity to analyze and evaluate problems in the light of principles and practices rather than feelings and attitudes.

The chart which follows provides a means whereby the personal qualities outlined above can be systematically treated and recorded. The evaluation of personal characteristics should normally be performed by one or more persons who fully understand the management analysis occupation and also by one or more representatives of the personnel office who are skilled in appraising the abilities of individuals.

The thoughtful and thorough evaluation of the applicant on the basis of the factors in this chart is an important aspect of the application of this standard. Also highly important are the experience and education requirements which must also be met. While the chart is designed to facilitate the appraisal of applicants in terms of the experience and education requirements stated above, the chart does not, of itself, constitute the standard.

(Inservice Placement Summary Evaluation Guide) Management Analyst GS-343-5/15 Summary Evaluation of Applicant's Personal Characteristics

Personal characteristics to be evaluated	Relative importance in job to be filed	DEGREE			HOW MEASURED		Recommended measuring devices (checkmark those used)
		Not demonstrated	Acceptable for position	Above average for position	E.g., written test interview, supervisory appraisal, etc.	Reason for degree assigned	
Ability to express self orally and in writing							Group oral, general interview
Ability to defend and sell products							Supervisory appraisal, group oral interview
Creativity in solving management problems							Supervisory appraisal, group oral, work product appraisal
Effectiveness in personal relationships with all levels of responsibility							Group oral, supervisory appraisal
Interest in the management process							General interview, reference inquiry
Ability to analyze complex problems							Group oral, work product appraisal

(Inservice Placement Summary Evaluation Guide) Management Analyst GS-343-5/15 Summary Evaluation of Applicant's Personal Characteristics **continued**

| Personal characteristics to be evaluated | Relative importance in job to be filed | DEGREE | | | HOW MEAS-URED | | Recommended measuring devices (checkmark those used) |
		Not dem-onstrated	Acceptable for posi-tion	Above av-erage for position	E.g., written test interview, supervisory appraisal, etc.	Reason for degree assigned	
Knowledge of management practices, theories, and techniques							Review of work history, work product appraisal, general interview, reference inquiry
Understanding role of management analysis in helping the organization achieve its goals							Supervisory appraisal, work product appraisal, general interview
Objectivity							Group oral, supervisory appraisal, reference inquiry, general interview
Other as required by position							

Use of the Summary

1. A summary sheet should be completed for each applicant. The summary is intended to be used as a guide to employing officials to aid in the evaluation and selection process. No criteria are provided for ranking applicants; however, agencies may utilize this summary sheet for ranking applicants, if desired.
2. For higher level positions (e.g., GS-13 and above), it is suggested that an extensive investigation of past experience be conducted as is feasible.
3. The format of this guide need not be followed but the information required should be made a matter of record in the personnel office.
4. Whenever practical, the specific experience which supports the evaluation of each factor should be recorded.
5. The measuring devices recommended in the chart above are not the only means by which personal characteristics may be evaluated. Those which are listed are most commonly used in the Federal service. However, there are other means of assessing personal characteristics which can be used when circumstances warrant. For example, it may be feasible to use employee self evaluations or appraisals by associates or fellow employees. In some cases, evaluation might be based in part on such techniques as having the applicant submit written solutions to specific problems of the types usually encountered by management analysts. As advances are made in the techniques of appraising personal characteristics of applicants for positions, such techniques should be used to the extent they may be applied to the management analysis occupation. In addition, agencies are encouraged to experiment in developing and improving methods of applicant appraisal, and in testing the validity of such techniques.

Evaluating Experience Gained in the Management Clerical and Assistance Series, GS-344

Experience as a management assistant (formerly technician) in the Federal service may be accepted as qualifying for the management analysis occupation when *all* of the following conditions are met:

A. The employee is being considered for reassignment from a management assistant position to a very similar management analysis position in the same grade;
B. The employee meets the basic qualification requirements for the management analysis position, i.e., the years of acceptable experience or substitutable education;

C. The duties, degree of responsibility, and subject matter of his management assistant position are sufficiently similar to the management analysis position to demonstrate clearly that the employee has the necessary background to perform satisfactorily the duties of the management analysis position to be filled; and

D. A determination has been made under the *Guide for Inservice Placement* above that the employee has the abilities, interest and capabilities to perform successfully the work of a management analysis position.

After lateral reassignment made under the above conditions the reassigned employee will be expected to demonstrate satisfactory performance in the management analysis position for a reasonable length of time before he is promoted to a higher grade management analysis position in accordance with the standard for the higher grade.

Physical Requirements

See part II, Physical Requirements, paragraph 3. In addition, applicants must possess emotional and mental stability.

Appendix

The following materials were published by the Women's Bureau, U.S. Department of Labor, Washington, D. C. From time to time these fact sheets and charts are updated from data furnished by the Bureau of the Census, U.S. Department of Commerce, and from other federal agencies and departments.

Pamphlets
Brief Highlights of Major Federal Laws on Sex Discrimination in Employment
Twenty Facts on Women Workers

Charts
Most women work because of economic need
Women are underrepresented as managers and skills craft workers
Most wives work to supplement family income
Fully employed women contined to earn less than fully employed men

U.S. Department of Labor   Office of the Secretary
Women's Bureau
Washington, D.C. 20210

BRIEF HIGHLIGHTS OF MAJOR FEDERAL LAWS
ON SEX DISCRIMINATION IN EMPLOYMENT

Equal Pay Act

This act prohibits pay discrimination because of sex. Men and women performing work in the same establishment under similar conditions must receive the same pay if their jobs require equal skill, effort, and responsibility. Differentials in pay based on a seniority or merit system, a system that measures earnings by quantity or quality of production, or any other factor other than sex are permitted.

Employers may not reduce the wage rate of any employee in order to eliminate illegal differentials. Labor organizations are prohibited from causing or attempting to cause employers to violate the act.

The act was approved in 1963 as an amendment to the Fair Labor Standards Act (FLSA) and applies to most workers in both the public and private sectors, including executive, administrative, and professional employees and outside sales personnel.1/

The Labor Department's Wage and Hour Division, which enforced the act until July 1979, officially interpreted its provisions to apply to "wages," which includes all remuneration for employment. Thus, the act prohibits discrimination in all employment-related payments, including overtime, uniforms, travel, retirement, and other fringe benefits. The Supreme Court has upheld the position that jobs of men and women need be only "substantially equal"--not identical--for purposes of comparison under the law.

The act is now enforced by the Equal Employment Opportunity Commission. Further information is available from district or area offices of the Commission or from:

Equal Employment Opportunity Commission
Washington, D.C. 20506

1/ A few categories of employees (such as those working in some small retail and service establishments) are specifically exempted from minimum wage and overtime requirements of the FLSA. On June 24, 1976, the U.S. Supreme Court declared unconstitutional provisions extending minimum wage and overtime coverage of the law to State and local government employees who are engaged in traditional governmental functions. The decision does not affect application of the equal pay provisions of the FLSA to employees of State and local governments.

Title VII of the Civil Rights Act of 1964, as Amended by the Equal Employment Opportunity Act of 1972 and the Pregnancy Discrimination Act

Title VII prohibits discrimination based on sex, as well as on race, color, religion, and national origin, in hiring or firing; wages; fringe benefits; classifying, referring, assigning, or promoting; extending or assigning use of facilities; training, retraining, or apprenticeships; or any other terms, conditions, or privileges of employment.

The law covers employers of 15 or more employees, employment agencies, labor organizations with 15 or more members, and labor-management apprenticeship programs. In 1972 educational institutions and State and local governments were brought under coverage (also, enforcement procedures for the affirmative program of equal opportunity in Federal employment--previously enunciated in Executive Order 11478--were substantially strengthened). Indian tribes are totally exempt as employers. Religious institutions or associations are exempt with respect to the employment of individuals of a particular religion in work connected with carrying on their activities. State and local elected officials, their personal staff, and policymaking appointees are excluded from the definition of "employee."

Title VII was amended by Public Law 95-555, approved October 31, 1978, to make clear that discrimination on the basis of pregnancy, childbirth, or related medical conditions constitutes unlawful sex discrimination. The amendment, referred to as the Pregnancy Discrimination Act, does not require employers to provide special benefits for pregnant employees or to institute new programs. It simply requires that women affected by pregnancy be treated the same for all employment-related purposes as other persons not so affected but similar in their ability or inability to work. Employers are not required to provide health insurance benefits for abortion, except where the life of the mother would be endangered if the fetus were carried to term, or except where medical complications have arisen from an abortion. However, the amendment specifically permits an employer to provide abortion benefits and does not otherwise affect bargaining agreements in regard to abortion. The amendment was effective immediately with respect to prohibiting policies such as refusal to hire or promote pregnant women; it was effective 180 days later (April 29, 1979) with respect to fringe benefit programs or funds or insurance programs in effect on the date of approval.

The Equal Employment Opportunity Commission (EEOC), which enforces title VII, has issued "Guidelines on Discrimination Because of Sex." These guidelines bar, among other discriminatory acts, hiring based on stereotyped characterization of the sexes, classification or labeling of "men's jobs" and "women's jobs," and advertising under male or female headings.

The guidelines declare that State laws which prohibit or limit the employment of women conflict with and are superseded by title VII. On the other hand, where State laws require benefits such as minimum wage and overtime pay for women only, an employer may not refuse to hire female applicants to avoid these

payments. Moreover, it must provide the same benefits for male employees.2/
Similar provisions apply to rest and meal periods and physical facilities.
However, if it can be proved that business necessity precludes providing these
benefits to both men and women, the employer must not provide them to members
of either sex.

In 1979 the EEOC revised the guidelines to bring them into conformity with the
Pregnancy Discrimination Act. Along with the revision, it published a series of
questions and answers that responded to urgent concerns raised by employers,
employees, unions, and insurers who had sought guidance as to their rights and
obligations under the law.

Other guidelines issued by the agency (either by itself or jointly with other Federal
civil rights agencies) deal with such subjects as voluntary affirmative action,
employee selection procedures, and sexual harassment.

Further information is available from district or area offices of the EEOC or from:

>Equal Employment Opportunity Commission
>Washington, D.C. 20506

Executive Order 11246, as Amended by Executive Order 11375

This order requires Federal contracts to include language by which contractors
pledge not to discriminate against any employee or applicant for employment
because of sex, race, color, religion, or national origin. The contractor must
further pledge to take affirmative action to ensure nondiscriminatory treatment.
Such action must include employment, upgrading, demotion, or transfer; recruitment or recruitment advertising; layoff or other forms of compensation; and
selection for training, including apprenticeship. Some contracts of $10,000 or less
are exempt by regulation.

The Secretary of Labor, who has overall enforcement responsibility for the order,
assigned administrative authority to the Office of Federal Contract Compliance
Programs (OFCCP).3/ Initially the OFCCP delegated compliance responsibility to
various Federal agencies, principally on the basis of industry classifications.
Under the President's Reorganization Plan No. 1 of 1978, the OFCCP assumed
total responsibility for enforcement on October 1, 1978.

2/ Of the two appeals courts that have ruled on this latter requirement, one
upheld and the other declared it an unconstitutional usurpation of State powers.
The Supreme Court has refused to hear an appeal from the latter decision. It
should be noted that most States which had minimum wage or overtime for women
only (including the one where the EEOC position was upheld by the appellate court)
have extended the benefit to men by legislative amendment. See State Labor Laws
in Transition: From Protection to Equal Status for Women, Women's Bureau
Pamphlet 15.

3/ The OFCCP also administers affirmative action programs of Federal
contractors with respect to handicapped workers, disabled veterans, and Vietnam
veterans.

110

Service or supply contractors or subcontractors that have 50 or more employees and a contract of $50,000 or more or Government bills of lading totaling $50,000 in any 12 month period must, within 120 days from the commencement of the contract, develop a written affirmative action compliance program for each of its establishments. The requirement also applies to financial institutions that have 50 or more employees and serve as a depository of Government funds or as an agent for issuing and paying U.S. savings bonds and savings notes in any amount. Regulations that became effective in December 1971 set forth the required contents of affirmative action programs for women and minorities. These include a review of the work force within each job group at a facility, establishment of goals and timetables for taking corrective steps where it is found that there are fewer women and minorities than would reasonably be expected by equal employment policy, and management responsibility for implementing and monitoring the policy. Techniques to improve recruitment and increase the flow of female or minority applicants are suggested. Goals are not to be rigid and inflexible quotas which must be met but rather targets reasonably attainable by application of every good faith effort.

Regulations providing a specific framework for construction contractors to carry out equal employment and affirmative action programs for women and minorities were published with an effective date of May 8, 1978.4/ Among the specific affirmative action steps required of such contractors are: ensuring that working sites are free of harassment, assigning two or more women to each construction project when possible, providing written notification to female recruitment sources and community organizations of employment opportunities, notifying OFCCP if the union referral process impedes efforts to meet affirmative action obligations, disseminating the equal employment opportunity policy within the company and in advertising, and actively recruiting women for apprenticeship or other training.

Also effective May 1978 OFCCP published a notice setting nationwide goals and timetables for the employment of women by contractors and subcontractors with a construction contract in excess of $10,000. The goals, which are nationwide, are 3.1 percent for the first year, 5 percent for the second year, and 6.9 percent for the third year. The goals are expressed in terms of hours of training and employment as a proportion of the total number of hours to be worked by each covered contractor's aggregate work force in each trade on all projects, either Federal or non-Federal.

4/ Until then programs for minorities only were in effect through "hometown plans" (voluntary agreements reached among contractors, unions, and representatives of the local minority community and approved by the OFCCP), imposed plans (which for the most part covered major metropolitan areas where there was substantial Federal or federally assisted construction, and applied only to projects in excess of $500,000), and special bid conditions (which applied to contractors working in certain high impact projects in areas not covered by hometown or imposed plans). The new regulations allowed hometown plans to remain in effect but eliminated the special bid conditions and imposed plans. Goals and timetables for minority workers established by these plans, however, continued to apply.

Sex discrimination guidelines issued by OFCCP effective June 1970 forbid advertising under male and female classifications, basing seniority lists on sex, denying jobs to qualified applicants because of State "protective" laws, making distinctions between married and unmarried persons of one sex only, terminating employees of one sex only upon reaching a certain age, and penalizing women in their conditions of employment because they require time away from work on account of childbearing. OFCCP has proposed amending these guidelines to conform to the Pregnancy Discrimination Act and to establish guidelines prohibiting sexual harassment.

Further information is available from:

> Office of Federal Contract Compliance Programs
> Employment Standards Administration
> U.S. Department of Labor
> Washington, D.C. 20210

Laws on Sex Discrimination in Employment Training

Access to appropriate training is a necessity if women are to be qualified for well-paying jobs. Among the steps the Federal Government has taken to enhance opportunities for women to receive such training are the following:

Amendments in 1976 to the Vocational Education Act mandated activities to eliminate sex bias, stereotyping, and discrimination in federally funded vocational education programs and required each State to employ a full-time sex equity coordinator to ensure the elimination of bias and occupational segregation in these programs. States are permitted to use Federal funds for vocational programs for certain categories of adult women, such as homemakers and part-time workers who are seeking full-time jobs and women who seek nontraditional employment.

The Comprehensive Employment and Training Act as reauthorized in 1978, prohibits sex discrimination with respect to participation in or employment in connection with any activity funded under the law. Moreover, prime sponsors (States, cities, counties, or combinations of general government units to whom most funds available under the law are allocated) must show in their annual plans the specific services planned for those who are experiencing severe handicaps in obtaining employment, including those who are displaced homemakers, or are 55 years of age or older, are single parents, or are women. All programs must contribute, to the maximum extent feasible, to occupational development, upward mobility, development of new careers, and overcoming sex-stereotyping (including procedures which will lead to skill development and job opportunities for participants in occupations traditionally limited to the opposite sex). Special national programs and activities mandated by the law also are targeted on groups deemed to face particular disadvantages in specific and general labor markets or occupations. Authorized research topics include the applicability of jobsharing, worksharing, and other flexible hours arrangements in various settings and the extent to which job and wage classification systems undervalue certain skills and responsibilities on the basis of the sex of persons who usually hold the positions.

Title IX of the 1972 Education Amendments states that no person in the United States shall, on the basis of sex, be excluded from participation in, be denied the benefits of, or be subjected to discrimination under any education program or activity receiving Federal financial assistance. It has been particularly effective in raising the proportion of women in law and medical schools.

The Women's Educational Equity Act of 1974 authorized activities at all levels of education to overcome sex-stereotyping and achieve equity for women. The program was reauthorized in 1978 and expanded to provide that appropriated funds over a specified level will be available for projects of local significance to help school districts and other institutions meet the requirements of title IX.

How Women Can Assert Their Job Rights

Problems in getting a job or in coping with the job situation often can be resolved through discussion with personnel officers or supervisors. In many work establishments, grievance procedures are available under collective bargaining agreements and formal equal employment opportunity programs. However, persons who believe that they are victims of illegal discrimination are entitled to file a complaint with the appropriate administrative agency.

Most States have laws that prohibit sex discrimination in private and/or public employment, and in some instances a Federal civil rights agency must defer to its State counterpart in the initial attempt to resolve complaints. Both State and Federal laws have limits on the time for filing charges of discrimination and on recovery of wages owed. Therefore, it is important that charges be filed promptly.

* * *

Single copies of the following related publications are available without charge upon request from the Women's Bureau, U.S. Department of Labor, Washington, D.C. 20210:

A Working Woman's Guide to Her Job Rights. Leaflet 55. January 1983.
1980 Handbook on Women Workers. (In press).
State Labor Laws in Transition: From Protection to Equal Status
    for Women. Pamphlet 15. 1976.
Publications of the Women's Bureau. Leaflet 10. 1982.

NOTE

This summary is intended for general information only. It does not carry the force of legal opinion.

August 1980

GPO 873-627

Facts on
Women Workers

U.S. Department of Labor
Office of the Secretary
Women's Bureau
1980

1. A majority of women work because of economic need. Nearly two-thirds of all women in the labor force in 1979 were single, widowed, divorced, or separated, or had husbands whose earnings were less than $10,000 (in 1978).

2. About 43 million women were in the labor force in 1979; they constituted more than two-fifths of all workers.

3. Sixty percent of all women 18 to 64--the usual working ages--were workers in 1979, compared with 88 percent of men. Fifty-one percent of all women 16 and over were workers. Labor force participation was highest among women 20 to 24.

4. The median age of women workers is 34 years.

5. Fifty-three percent of all black women were in the labor force in 1979 (5.0 million); they accounted for nearly half of all black workers.

6. Forty-seven percent of Spanish-origin women were in the labor force in March 1979 (2.0 million); they accounted for 39 percent of all Spanish-origin workers.

7. Women accounted for nearly three-fifths of the increase in the civilian labor force in the last decade--about 13 million women compared with more than 9 million men.

8. More than one-fourth of all women workers held part-time jobs in 1979.

9. In 1977 the average woman could expect to spend 27.6 years of her life in the work force, compared with 38.3 years for men.

10. The more education a woman has the greater the likelihood she will seek paid employment. Among women with 4 or more years of college, about 2 out of 3 were in the labor force in 1979.

11. The average woman worker is as well educated as the average man worker; both have completed a median of 12.6 years of schooling.

12. The number of working mothers has increased more than tenfold since the period immediately preceding World War II, while the number of working women more than tripled. Fifty-five pecent of all mothers with children under 18 years (16.6 million) were in the labor force in 1979; 45 percent of. mothers with preschool children were working.

13. The 6.0 million working mothers 1/ with preschool children in 1979 had 7.2 million children under age 6, compared with 5.1 million working mothers with 6.1 million children under 6 years of age in 1974.

114

14. The unemployment rate was lowest for adult white men (20 and over) and highest for young black women (16 to 19) in 1979:

Adults	Percent	Teenagers	Percent
White men	3.6	White men	13.9
White women	5.0	White women	13.9
Hispanic men	5.7	Hispanic men	17.4
Hispanic women	8.9	Hispanic women	21.3
Black men	9.1	Black men	34.0
Black women	10.8	Black women	39.2

15. Women workers are concentrated in low paying dead end jobs. As a result, the average woman worker earns only about three-fifths of what a man does, even when both work full time year round. The median wage or salary income of year-round full-time workers in 1978 was lowest for minority-race 2/ women-- $8,996. For white women it was $9,578; minority men, $12,885; and white men, $16,194.

The median earnings of full-time year-round women farm workers were $2,360; private household workers, $2,830; sales workers, $7,644; and clerical workers, $9,158.

16. Fully employed women high school graduates (with no college) had less income on the average than fully employed men who had not completed elementary school--$9,769 and $10,474, respectively, in 1978. Women with 4 years of college also had less income than men with only an 8th grade education--$12,347 and $12,965, respectively.

17. Among all families, about 1 out of 7 was maintained by a woman in 1979 compared with about 1 out of 10 in 1969; 40 percent of black families were maintained by women. Of all women workers, about 1 out of 6 maintained a family; about 1 out of 4 black women workers maintained a family.

18. Among all poor families, half were maintained by women in 1979; about 3 out of 4 poor black families were maintained by women. In 1969 about one-third (35 percent) of all poor families were maintained by women and 51 percent of poor minority 3/ families were maintained by women.

1/ Includes never married mothers.

2/ "Minority races" refers to all races other than white. Blacks constitute about 90 percent of persons other than white in the United States. Spanish-origin persons are generally included in the white population; about 93 percent of the Spanish-origin population is white.

3/ Data on black families are not available for 1969.

Source: U.S. Department of Commerce, Bureau of the Census; U.S. Department of Health and Human Services (formerly Department of Health, Education, and Welfare), National Center for Social Statistics; U.S. Department of Labor, Bureau of Labor Statistics and Employment and Training Administration.

19. It is frequently the wife's earnings which raise a family out of poverty. In husband-wife families in 1979, 14.8 percent were poor when the wife did not work; 3.8 percent when she was in the labor force. Of all wives who worked in 1979, the median contribution was more than one-fourth of the total family income. Among those who worked year round full time, it was nearly two-fifths. Among black families, the median contribution of working wives was one-third of the total family income.

20. Women were 80 percent of all clerical workers in 1979 but only 6 percent of all craft workers (women were about 3 percent of all apprentices as of December 1978); 62 percent of service workers but only 43 percent of professional and technical workers; and 63 percent of retail sales workers but only 25 percent of nonfarm managers and administratrators.

Most women work because of economic need

Women in the Labor Force, March 1979

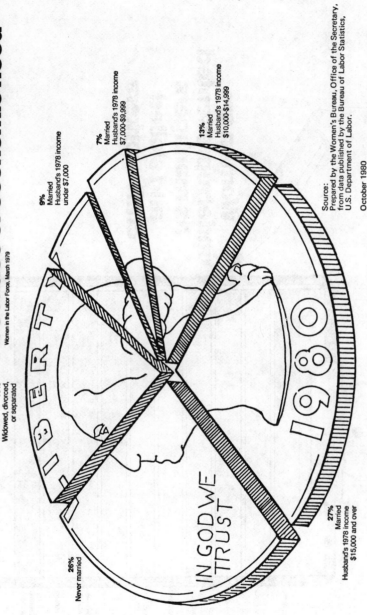

9%
Married
Husband's 1978 income
under $7,000

7%
Married
Husband's 1978 income
$7,000-$9,999

13%
Married
Husband's 1978 income
$10,000-$14,999

19%
Widowed, divorced,
or separated

26%
Never married

27%
Married
Husband's 1978 income
$15,000 and over

Source:
Prepared by the Women's Bureau, Office of the Secretary, from data published by the Bureau of Labor Statistics, U.S. Department of Labor.

October 1980

117

Women are underrepresented as managers and skilled craft workers

Occupation	Percent
All occupations	42%
Craft workers	6%
Managers	25%
Nonretail sales workers	26%
Operatives	32%
Professional workers	43%
Service workers	62%
Retail sales workers	63%
Clerical workers	80%
Private household workers	98%

Percent of total workers

Source:
Prepared by the Women's Bureau, Office of the Secretary, from 1979 annual averages data published by the Bureau of Labor Statistics, U.S. Department of Labor.

October 1980

Most wives work to supplement family income

Family income in 1978

Category	Percent
All women workers	28.1
Under $3,000	29.7
$3,000-$4,999	21.9
$5,000-$6,999	23.5
$7,000-$9,999	26.9
$10,000-$12,999	26.3
$13,000-$14,999	25.6
$15,000-$19,999	26.8
$20,000-$24,999	26.9
$25,000-$34,999	27.2
$35,000-$49,999	25.2
$50,000 and over	17.6
Year-round full-time workers	37.6

Percent

Source:
Prepared by the Women's Bureau, Office of the Secretary,
from data published by the Bureau of Labor Statistics,
U.S. Department of Labor.

October 1980

Fully employed women continue to earn less than fully employed men

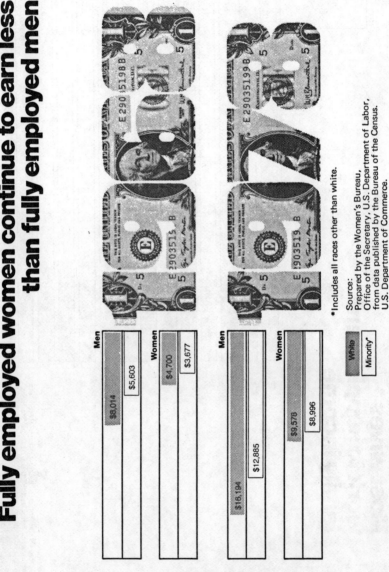

Men

$8,014
$5,603

Women

$4,700
$3,677

Men

$16,194
$12,885

Women

$9,578
$8,996

White
Minority*

*Includes all races other than white.

Source:
Prepared by the Women's Bureau,
Office of the Secretary, U.S. Department of Labor,
from data published by the Bureau of the Census.
U.S. Department of Commerce.

October 1980

120

Breaking the Barriers
for Women in Government:
An Historical Perspective

On December 4, 1961, President John F. Kennedy issued Executive Order 10980 establishing the President's Commission on the Status of Women. This was the first time in recent history a president of the United States initiated a program drawing attention to the role of women in our society.

The findings of this Presidential Commission provided the basis for future presidents to take constructive steps to implement the Commission's recommendations, among which were employment policies and practices of the United States government affecting employed women.

In the course of its study, the Commission uncovered the existence of a statute that allowed the federal government discretion in hiring men only or women only, as they saw fit. Not surprisingly, except for jobs typically performed by women, such as secretary, typist, or clerk, agencies opted for the appointment of men.

This prompted President Kennedy to issue a memorandum to the heads of all departments and agencies informing them that he had directed the Civil Service Commission ". . . to review pertinent personnel policies and practices affecting the employment of women and to work . . . to assure that selection for any career position is made solely on the basis of individual merit and fitness."

But the mills of the gods grind slowly. It took three years before Congress repealed the discriminatory statute in 1965.

In 1963, the President's Commission on the Status of Women completed its study and submitted a published report in which, among many other recommendations, it suggested establishment of an Interdepartmental Committee to be composed of cabinet officers and a Citizens Advisory Committee composed of private citizens to ensure continued advancement of the status of women in all sectors of society. Unhesitatingly, both were established.

In April, 1964, at a White House reception honoring newly appointed women to major federal positions, President Lyndon B. Johnson, casting a benevolent gaze upon the group, said

> We can open, and we are opening, the doors of public service and I think this is going to influence some other sectors as well. My whole aim in promoting women and picking out more women to serve in this Administration is to underline our profound belief that we can waste no talent, we can frustrate no creative power, we can neglect no skill in our search for an open and just and challenging society. There is no place for discrimination of any kind in American life. There must be places for citizens who can think and create and act.

In October, 1967, President Johnson issued an Executive Order that, for the first time, outlawed employment discrimination on the basis of sex as well as race, color, creed, and national origin. This Order provided the impetus to formalize a Federal Women's Program by directing the Civil Service Commission (now Office of Personnel Management) to develop guidelines, and provide leadership and the tools necessary to implement the program.

In January, 1968, the Civil Service Commission issued to all agencies a "Definition of a Positive Federal Women's Program" that left no doubt that an Equal Employment Opportunity program for women had to be initiated by top management and supported by operating officials at all levels.

Despite this proclamation by the President of the United States, the path for women eager to utilize their full potential was still strewn with obstacles. During the period 1963 to 1966, several pieces of legislation had been enacted aimed at removing barriers to equal opportunity for women: The Equal Pay Act, the Higher Education Facilities Act, the Civil Rights Act, the Social Security Act of 1965 establishing Medicare, the Elementary and Secondary Education Act, and the Fair Employment Standards Act, amended in 1966.

When the Interdepartmental Committee on the Status of Women submitted a report of its five-year study to the President in 1968, it asked and answered its own question: "What are the prospects for American women in the years ahead?" The answer: "For some—far too many—the freedom to engage more fully and productively in American society is still limited by social forces too large for them as individuals to control . . ."

When President Nixon took his turn at the helm of the ship of state, he appointed a Task Force on Women's Rights and Responsibilities to carry on previous presidential efforts to facilitate the entry of women into the mainstream of society.

This Task Force submitted its findings to the President in December, 1969. Like the Interdepartmental Committee of the Johnson era, the group found little cause for elation. Its conclusions, summarized in a letter of transmittal to the President, stated in part:

> Women do not seek special privileges. They do seek equal rights. They do wish to assume their full responsibilities.

With specific reference to the role of women in federal service, the Task Force decried the paucity of women in responsible positions and recommended:

> The President should appoint more women to positions of top responsibility in all branches of the Federal Government, to achieve a more equitable ratio of men and women. Cabinet and agency heads should be directed to issue firm instructions that qualified women receive equal consideration in hiring and promotions.
> The present pace of appointments of women to high Federal positions should be accelerated, to reflect their numerical strength more realistically, and as an incentive and symbol of the Administration's commitment.
> In making appointments the 'showcase' approach or tokenism should be avoided. Women should not be confined to the so-called distaff area but brought into the dynamics of policy development.

The existing bank of qualified women economists, lawyers, politicians, jurists, educators, scientists, physicians, writers, and administrators has the intellectual capacity to meet the most exacting demands.

What was the response to all these recommendations? Disappointing! In 1973, the President's Advisory Council on Management submitted its report on "Women in Government" to the White House, noting a continuing lack of commitment to advancing women in government. It concluded:

> Within the Federal Government the attitudes of both men and women concerning the role of working women interfere with efforts to implement an equal employment opportunity program. This is a serious problem. Managers need to be aware that underutilization of womanpower is a waste to the Government, not only of human potential but also of dollars and cents.
>
> Closely allied to the attitudinal problem is the lack of involvement of top managers in the program, and the lack of commitment of resources. The program for women has not been adequately funded or staffed within the agencies or at the Civil Service Commission.
>
> Implementation of the program at the agency level is unsatisfactory. Line management must be held accountable for carrying out affirmative action plans. Responsibility must be placed with those who make the final decisions on hiring and promoting.
>
> The Federal Government has made a good beginning in its effort to remedy the underutilization of its women employees. It is important not to lose the momentum already gained.

Time marches on! In June, 1976, the National Commission on the Observance of International Women's Year 1975, appointed by President Ford, submitted its report entitled " ... to Form a More Perfect Union."

One section of the report dealing with federal civil service clearly indicates there can be no letup in the drive for recognition and acceptance of women's potential. For example, by its own admission, the Civil Service Commission stated:

> In the Federal Government today, women comprise about 35 percent of full-time white-collar employees. In the mid-level range, GS-9 through GS-12, women represent 18.9 percent; at the senior levels, GS-13 to GS-18, they represent only 4.7 percent. The five largest professional groupings are nursing, educational and vocational training, library science, medical technology, and accounting. There is evidence of some growth in such categories as internal revenue agents, health

sciences, medical officers, and attorneys. Some recent career break-throughs allow women to serve as secret service and narcotic agents, border patrol, and postal inspectors. But the fact remains that of all women employed by Federal Government, only 2 percent are at GS-13 or higher.

While glaring, overt discrimination is slowly being dealt with, much remains to be done to ferret out the disparate treatment of women which exists in the government's personnel management system. The Commission is stressing ways to change attitudes of personnel and program managers and to motivate women themselves.

The report included statements from several federal agencies reaffirming the need for continuous monitoring of efforts to bring women into the mainstream of public service:

> Some awareness has been increased by such activities of the Federal Women's Program as seminars, council meetings, bulletins. The Program has reached the female work force and has touched some of the male work force. However, there is a great need for sensitivity training in order that all our employees may learn to relate to each other.
>
> For things to improve for women, management must sincerely and completely commit itself.
>
> We have made some gains in the past several years in our employment of women in management positions. We view our gains to date as only the beginning, however.

It must be clear to the reader by now that the federal government is not galloping toward the twenty-first century as a pacesetter for women in the work force.

Not to be one-upped by his predecessors, President Carter created the Interdepartmental Task Force on Women in April, 1978. Its mission was " . . . to review federal programs, policies and initiatives for the promotion of full equality for American women." The Task Force was chaired by an Assistant to the President with an office in the White House and with ready access to the President.

So once again the wheels were greased and spinning. With renewed incentive, Federal Women's Program Managers were encouraged to gather data on areas of underutilization of women and to recommend appropriate action to correct deficiencies. Though not all management officials throughout government were persuaded, on the whole, the response was promising. Women, especially in mid-level grades, began to move up the career ladder.

To aid Federal Women's Program Managers in planning and carrying out their responsibilities, the Office of the Federal Women's Program at the Office of Personnel Management issued a "Handbook for Federal Women's Program Managers," which outlined step by step the duties and responsibilities of those responsible for executing the program.

Indirectly it served another purpose. It informed heads of agencies that here was a program with teeth and they had better bite into it. Some responded accordingly. Others gave it lipservice.

In most agencies the Federal Women's Program is but one of three components within the Office of Civil Rights (some call it the Office of Equal Employment Opportunity). The other two components are concerned with employment and advancement opportunities for minorities and Hispanics. Only the Directors of the Offices of Civil Rights have direct access to senior management. With this kind of filtering system, issues of concern to women do not always reach the ears of policymakers.

By the end of his term, while his scorecard was not spectacular, it was impressive. According to the report of the Interdepartmental Task Force on Women, January 1980, President Carter had appointed more women to high-level government jobs than any other president in history. Of 2,110 high-level appointments, 22 percent (436) were women. Among them were twenty-eight federal judges; four cabinet officers (Secretaries of Health, Education and Welfare (HEW); Housing and Urban Development (HUD); Department of Education; and Department of Commerce); thirteen ambassadors to foreign countries; three cabinet undersecretaries; twenty assistant secretaries; five heads of agencies and commissions; and several hundred policy-making executives throughout the federal establishment.

Typically, such appointments are political in nature and carry the risk of termination when a president leaves office. When Carter lost his bid for reelection, all of these women, except federal judges, joined the ranks of the unemployed.

I talked with a number of these women since they lost their prestigious positions, and not one regrets the experience. On the contrary, they knew they were taking a risk which, in the long run, would better equip them for responsible and challenging positions elsewhere. Many already are gainfully employed and enjoying yet another career challenge.

With this historical perspective, you can readily understand why it is of particular importance to career-minded women to be alert to the obstacles on which they may stub their toes in the quest for success. Militancy is not the solution. Preparedness, awareness, perseverance, patience, and dogged determination are the vital characteristics of an achiever.

With the arrival of the Reagan administration in January, 1981, the momentum gained by women in the past decade ground to a halt. For the first time in recent history a President of the United States declared open opposition to a Constitutional Amendment for Equal Rights, an amendment that does no more than guarantee equal *legal* rights for women as well as men.

The domino effect of this negative attitude has been further evident in the lack of support for a dynamic federal women's program throughout federal agencies.

In 1982, in response to a query about the future of the program, one Federal Women's Program Manager was told by a newly appointed top-level official to advise women to go home where they belonged and raise babies, because that was "their God-given responsibility."

Added to this distressing view of women in the work force, massive budget cuts, reductions in force, and reorganizations have been ordered throughout the government. Several agencies are destined for the chopping block. First to go was the Community Services Administration, abolished in September, 1981. Next in line President Reagan proposed abolishing the Department of Education and the Department of Energy. All told, close to 100,000 federal jobs are slated for elimination within the next three years. Given this chaotic situation, affirmative action programs have a low priority. What happens to the Federal Women's Program in the foreseeable future is anybody's guess.

Added to these woes, an ultraconservative Congress, many of whom were elected in 1980, share the President's views. In fact, some members of this august body had drafted legislation designed to put women "in their place"—traditional family roles, they called it—the kitchen and the nursery.

"It's almost impossible to get into civil service at this time," a high-level OPM official told me in the summer of 1981, "there are so few openings and so many people with long-term career status being fired."

So the immediate outlook for employment or advancement, particularly for women in federal service, is less than favorable. But, take heart! Before you give up the quest for federal employment, let me don my Pollyanna cloak for a moment and gaze into the crystal ball I have been eyeing for the past three decades.

In a democracy such as ours, no administration stays in power forever. Presidents hold office for four years. Members of the House of Representatives stand for election every two years. Senators serve six-year terms. However, one-third of the Senate is up for election every two years. True, there is no limit to the number of times representatives and senators may be reelected. By the same token, they may also be voted out of office by an informed constituency that disapproves of their performance.

Though women are viewed as a powerless group in our society, they can wield considerable power at the ballot box. An educated, informed electorate can make a difference. And that applies to you.

With 60 percent of American women between the ages of eighteen and sixty-four in the work force, they have much to gain or lose by the actions of the Congress of the United States, as well as by the President. Therefore it behooves every career-minded woman to learn the voting record of her Congressional representative and senators on all issues. She must become aware of the political process in order to protect the gains women have made in the past decade and not be forced once again into second-class citizenship.

So, while Federal Women's Program Managers may have had their wings clipped in 1982, rendering them impotent to advance the cause of women, the fact remains, thousands of women still are employed in government and will continue to be.

After the massive reductions in force are completed, agencies will find themselves unable to complete their missions with such reduced staffs. And before you realize it, the recruitment cycle will begin, albeit on a limited scale. Historically, that has been the pattern.

In the interim, it would be wise to prepare for a career in an occupation that is not overloaded. Science, engineering, financial management, computer specializations are areas that will offer the greatest opportunities in the foreseeable future.

The "Occupational Outlook Quarterly" and the "Occupational Outlook Handbook," both published by the Bureau of Labor Statistics, Department of Labor, are bellweathers of anticipated work force needs, in the public as well as the private sector. The examination announcements issued by the Office of Personnel Management provide clues to needs in the federal government. Checking vacancy announcements posted on bulletin boards in federal agencies is yet another source of information. The most effective avenue, of course, is to visit the personnel office in the agency of your choice with a well-prepared resume and inquire about job opportunities. Better still, if you have friends or relatives in government, ask them to be on the lookout for opportunities in their respective agencies and then arrange for interviews with the specific hiring officials. Many Federal Women's Program Managers are in a position to offer suggestions and advice. Find out who they are and get to know them.

Though the job market seems dismal in 1983, change is inevitable. Just remember, the parade passes by every four years.

5

The Role of Mentors, Sponsors, and Networks

Whenever the subject of mentors comes up in a group discussion, there's always someone in the crowd who says, "Humpf, I never had a mentor, I got where I am completely on my own." Well, don't you believe it! Whether in business, government, or politics, no one "makes it" on his or her own.

In October, 1981, the press reported that the twenty-five-year-old daughter of the Secretary of State was hired as a staff assistant to the associate director of a major program division of another federal agency at a salary of $18,585 per annum. In the next paragraph it reported the appointment of the thirty-four-year-old son of Secretary of Defense to a high-level position in the New York office of the same agency at a salary of $44,500. Later we learn that the twenty-eight-year-old son of a well-known conservative columnist was appointed to a position on the White House staff.

Many sons and daughters of famous movie stars and legitimate stage actors and actresses have gotten their "breaks" in the world of make-believe on the strength of a parent's reputation or connections, while hundreds of talented, would-be actors pounded the pavements looking for jobs.

Look at the Ford Motor Company dynasty—generations of sons and grandsons have run the corporation. The *Washington Post* in Washington, D. C. is yet another example: handed down from father to son-in-law, then to daughter upon the death of the son-in-law, and now to the daughter's son.

Whatever label you put on it—mentor, sponsor, benefactor—it is important to have connections, someone somewhere, whether inside or out of the organization, with the power to affect your future.

A study reported in the *Harvard Business Review* (January-February, 1979) quotes the Chairman and Chief Executive Officer of the Jewel Companies as saying ". . . everyone who succeeds has had a mentor or mentors."

In this same study of 1,250 executives who responded to a questionnaire, two-thirds reported having had a mentor or sponsor, and one-third of them had had two or more mentors.

Nationally less than 1 percent of corporate executives are women. So it is not surprising that only twenty-eight were invited to respond to this same questionnaire. Not all complied. But the replies of those who did are worth noting:

> Women tend to have more mentors than men, averaging three sponsors to the men's two. While women executives had female mentors more often than men did, seven in 10 of the women's mentors were male.

Most of the women respondents stated their mentor relationships were formed ". . . in the work setting . . . during the sixth to tenth years of their careers," which was about the period when they decided to pursue a "career" rather than just "work."

In 1981, another study was conducted, this time concentrating on the relationship of male mentors of women (*Harvard Business Review*, March-April, 1981). Participating were thirty women executives from twenty-seven companies.

Among the findings: ". . . at lower levels in organizations women typically need more encouragement than their male counterparts, at higher levels mentors of women have to spend more time 'selling' their proteges."

One mentor commented that his principal effort was to convince those higher up about a woman's ability to take on greater responsibilities. He stated, "when you are trying to present a woman to your superiors, you often feel you have to explain everything, and you try to put the gender issue right out of their minds."

Selling job! Explain everything! Gender issue! Oh, how those words struck home! Let me share with you a personal experience that ultimately resulted in a mentor-sponsor relationship that gave my career a boost. It could happen to you.

A number of years ago, after interviewing me for a position on his staff and deciding I had the credentials he sought, Tom Brown approached his division director and announced that he had found just the person he wanted to fill the vacancy in his branch.

"Great!" said the director, Bob Smith, "Is he anyone I know?"

To which Mr. Brown replied, "He's a *she*."

Somewhat taken aback, Bob Smith said, "You've got to be crazy, Tom, to hire a woman for that job. Did you tell her about all the travel involved?"

Not waiting for answers, Smith continued, "You know how women are . . . they are never free to travel, especially if they are married. Is she married?"

"Yes, she is," Brown managed to get in while Smith caught his breath, "and she knows all about the required travel."

Shaking his head in dismay, the director said, "You'll be sorry," and repeated, "You know how women are—they always want you to carry their luggage and I hate that, I even hate to carry my own."

"Well," Brown responded, "she strikes me as the type who wouldn't ask for favors."

"O.K.," said the director, with a shrug of the shoulders, "It's your shop and I don't want to dictate whom you should hire, but I'm telling you," wagging a long index finger at Mr. Brown, "you'll regret it."

I was hired. Within a few weeks after reporting for duty, the director, my boss, and I were scheduled to visit one of our field offices to discuss an important program and also to introduce me to the people I would be working with in the future.

On a Monday afternoon I was told to be at the airport, ready for departure at 8 A.M. the next day. I did not realize at the time I was being "tested." This short notice was the director's idea.

After making hasty arrangements for my twelve-year-old daughter and my husband to fend for themselves for a couple of days, I dutifully arrived at the airport bright and early with a small carry-on suitcase. Having traveled extensively on official business in prior years, I had learned the art of traveling light.

As we headed for the ladder to board the plane, the director turned to me and asked if he could carry my bag. "Oh, no," I replied, "thanks just the same, but I always carry my own luggage."

At that moment Mr. Brown burst out laughing and turning to the director said, "What did I tell you!"

I was baffled by this episode, wondering what I had said or done to warrant this outburst of laughter. Once seated on the plane, I turned to Mr. Brown, who sat next to me while the director sat across the aisle, and asked what that was all about. He told me the story about the director's objection to hiring a woman—especially a married woman.

While I shared his amusement, I couldn't help wondering what my future would have been in that organization had I played the role of "the weaker sex" and handed my suitcase to the director.

From that point on, my boss became my mentor. He was convinced I would pull my oar no matter how rocky the boat. He told me all about the people I would be dealing with in our various field offices from coast to coast and what to look for in coping with personalities and issues that would arise. Gradually he delegated more and more responsibility to me and left me on my own to solve problems. Yet he made it clear that any time I wanted to discuss a problem, try out a new idea, or propose a change in policy, his door was open and he was available for a dialogue.

A couple of years later a new position was established in our division and the search was on for someone to head this newly created section. By this time I had been fully accepted as a member of the team, even by the director, and gender differences never interfered with work assignments. So when my boss approached the director, suggesting he offer me the new position, he did so without hesitation. I leaped at the prospect of this challenging assignment and never regretted the move. It was a chance to prove myself.

Too few women get the opportunity to tackle something new, especially a job in which they would be responsible for developing and subsequently implementing a program that would affect an entire organization. I've known women to turn down or avoid applying for such positions for fear of failure. If women really want to get ahead, they must be prepared to take risks. Sure, mistakes will be made along the way, but men make mistakes too. What it takes is self-confidence and a positive outlook. Most mistakes can be corrected. That's part of the secret of success.

There are relatively few women in senior-level positions, in government or in the private sector. With so few role models to emulate, having a mentor or mentors is vital to the woman with career aspirations.

Some authorities on organizational development use the terms "mentor" and "sponsor" interchangeably. But there is a difference. A mentor can be your immediate supervisor, a peer, a subordinate, or someone one or more levels higher in your organizational chain of command. A sponsor, more often than not, is someone in a position of power in the organization who can legitimately bypass all others in the hierarchy to proclaim your virtues for a particular position, someone who is willing to go to bat for you. A sponsor also could be someone outside of your agency or corporation who knows you, has confidence in your ability, and wouldn't hesitate to recommend you to someone in authority within your organization for a particular job.

That's where networking comes in.

Men have been networking all their working lives. Social clubs like Lions, Rotary, and Civitans; country clubs; church groups; professional organizations; the "lunch-bunch"; and the golf course, are some of the places where men meet for a variety of reasons, not the least of which is the opportunity to exchange business cards, talk about what they do for a living, encourage the exchange of business services among their "brothers," and make friends. Often this "old-boys network" is the path to better job opportunities.

Another classic example of the network in action is evidenced each time a president of the United States is elected. Hundreds of political appointments become available with each new administration. Who gets these choice positions, from cabinet officers to secretaries, and all those in-betweens? Friends and friends of friends, campaign workers, and financial contributors, as noted earlier in this chapter.

In this instance, I regret to say, the "buddy" system does not always work in the best interest of the government. Too many political appointees have neither the qualifications nor commitment to public service and are the cause of lowered employee morale and productivity. But, that's the way the system works.

One reason for belonging to a group—a network—is enlightened self-interest. And there's nothing wrong with that.

Women have been active in civic, social, educational, and professional organizations for generations; yet they seldom viewed their activities as networking for self-interest. "'Tis the nature of women," say the sociologists, to nurture others rather than themselves. Maybe so. But in the past decade, working women have begun to break out of their cocoons, spread their wings, and march forward in quest of an equal opportunity.

With more than half of the women in America over the age of sixteen in the labor force, and their ranks increasing at the rate of about a million women a year, it becomes increasingly evident that if women are to advance to positions of power and prestige, they will have to link arms and learn to "play the game" as men have done for generations. They must develop their own "buddy" systems to help other women further their careers.

One reason the wage gap between men and women is so overwhelming is that too few women are in positions of power to effect change. On average, women's earnings are only 59 percent of men's. The gap narrows somewhat in professional positions but gross disparities remain, despite the fact that in many occupations women's academic credentials are superior to those of their male colleagues.

Women also are becoming more sophisticated and knowledgeable about the ground rules for success. No one is nurturing the nurturers. There are no fairy godmothers (or godfathers, for that matter) prepared to extend a hand in the climb up the career ladder. Aware that they are on their own in a highly competitive market, women have begun to adopt some of the better tactics so effectively employed by men—developing and using networks.

Networks come in all sizes and shapes. Some are formal, structured, dues-paying organizations with clearly defined policies and criteria for membership. Others are loosely organized, casual, but equally effective.

I belong to a couple of networks but one of my favorites is a group that meets on the same day and week each month for lunch and conversation. Membership is limited to 100 professional women who occupy high-level positions or are self-employed. Among them are doctors, lawyers, dentists, stockbrokers, newspaper columnists, consultants, educators, corporate lobbyists, retail business owners, members of Congressional staffs, women in federal government, and others in a variety of occupations.

At each luncheon whoever knows of a good job opportunity announces it to the group. Interested members can follow up on such leads or refer their friends or colleagues as potential candidates. At times a member will inform the group of her interest in a career change and offer copies of her resume for distribution to other members who may be in a position to help her relocate.

Often there is a speaker; sometimes it is a member of the group who shares information about her profession, such as a stockbroker advising about trends in the financial world; a dentist demonstrating new techniques in cosmetic dentistry; lobbyists informing the group of their current efforts to persuade the Congress to act favorably on legislation affecting women.

Other times we have no speaker. Instead we mix and mingle. Just meeting and talking with women of diverse backgrounds gives one insights into the kinds of work women are doing and the skills needed for their respective jobs. The atmosphere is very supportive. Several members have succeeded in finding new positions through the sponsorship of their colleagues. This is networking at its best.

Professional organizations provide an excellent source for networking. Almost any professional organization you can name has chapters in cities and towns up and down the nation. The American Society for Training and Development (ASTD), for example, has 20,000 members spread out among 122 chapters. The International Personnel Management Association (IPMA), with forty-six chapters, has approximately 4,000 members. The American Society for Public Administration (ASPA), an organization dedicated to improving management in the public sector at the federal, state, and local levels, has more than 17,000 members in 110 chapters worldwide.

Mention a profession and you will find it has an association for its peers. To list but a few more: The American Medical Association, American Management Associations, American Bar Association, National Bar Association (for black attorneys), Federal Women's Bar Association (for women attorneys in federal service), Society of Engineers, Society of Women Engineers, American Psychological Association, American Psychiatric Association, Association of Government Accountants, International Association for Personnel Women. There are hundreds more.

Not to be overlooked are organizations concerned with "women's issues." The Women's Equity Action League (WEAL) and Federally Employed Women (FEW) are two of the major groups that share a common theme—improving education and employment opportunities for women. WEAL's programs encompass the universe of women, while FEW's programs are directed toward women in federal employment. In both of these organizations members work in a multitude of different occupations but they are united in their efforts to overcome the barriers to career advancement, that is, the elimination of sex discrimination in employment. They share another common bond—networking.

I cannot overemphasize the value of expanding your external networks by getting involved in professional organizations. But it's not enough merely to be a dues-paying member and attend an occasional meeting. It is important to volunteer for committee or task force assignments and to run for elected office. Become known among your peers as a "do-er." Build a reputation by demonstrating leadership skills, communications skills, or whatever else you can do to win friends and influence people. If you are looking to get ahead, you need not wear a "for sale" sign around your neck, but keep your antenna up through your organization activities, and watch and listen for the right time and the right person to whom you can drop a hint about your career aspirations. You never know when it may pay off. I can attest to that from personal experience.

At a professional personnel association luncheon one day, I was seated next to a woman I had not previously met. We introduced ourselves and told each other how and where we earned our bread and butter. On learning that she was responsible for recruiting senior-level managers, I mentioned that I was considering looking for a career change because I felt the position I held at that time offered limited career advancement.

A couple of weeks passed before I received a telephone call from this luncheon partner telling me of a position in another agency that she thought might interest me. I thanked her and promptly followed up on the lead. As you may have guessed, since I'm telling of the experience, I landed the job. It was one of the most exciting changes I had ever made. I found myself in a leadership role that subsequently opened other doors to advancement.

I called my benefactor and invited her to be my guest for lunch so I could again express my appreciation for her efforts.

About a year later she telephoned me to talk about a friend who was looking for a career change and asked if I could help her. I interviewed the woman, found her highly qualified for a position in my agency that I knew would become available in a couple of months. I "sold" her to the operating official, who relied heavily on my judgment of people. In due time she was hired and turned out to be an excellent employee. So the agency got a top-notch employee and I was able to repay a favor. Today we call it networking.

On another occasion, at a professional organization luncheon, I was seated next to a woman I had known casually some years before. In the course of getting reacquainted I learned she was a program director in the continuing education department at a local college. She invited me to be a guest lecturer at one of her programs. This led to my being invited to teach a career development course at the college, which I did for several semesters.

Always have a current SF-171 and a resume handy. Update it periodically. Frequently I receive telephone calls telling me about job openings and asking me to refer people for them. Often when I pass the information along to women I know are potential candidates, they reply, "Oh, I don't have a current application on hand and couldn't possibly have one ready by the deadline." Too bad. Some of the best opportunities have been lost for failure to be able to act promptly. When opportunity knocks, better be prepared to open the door.

Have some business cards made. They are an invaluable source for networking. Exchange cards with people you meet at professional meetings, at informal luncheons, or other gatherings. Cards need not be elaborate or expensive. A simple card with your name, address, and telephone numbers—home and business—will suffice. If you are employed, include job title and name of employer.

One organization in which I've been active places a large punch bowl at the registration desk at each monthly meeting. As people register for the meeting, they drop a business card in the punch bowl. After the group is seated, the bowl is passed around and each person draws a card. The purpose is to encourage members to telephone the person whose card they have drawn and arrange to meet for lunch or dinner and get acquainted. It is a great way to broaden your network. These meetings draw between 75 and 200 people each month. It would be humanly impossible to get to know everyone.

After years of exchanging cards with people from all over the country, I couldn't begin to remember where I met them, what we talked about, and what, if any, mutual interests we may have had. So before I put the cards in my alphabetical file, I note on the back where and when we met, what we talked about, and whether any of them could be a resource for job opportunities for my clients or colleagues or for other information I might need at some future date. As a result, I have become a walking encyclopedia of "who's who." When my eighteen-inch long file box becomes full, I purge it; removing cards of people I have had no occasion to contact or refer others to for three or more years.

This is the way men have operated for years, broadening their "old-boys" network. It's high time women adopt the same tactics and reach out to help other women up the ladder through the "new women's" networks.

Federal Women
Speak Out

The primary focus of this book has been on getting started and climbing the career ladder. So I thought you would like to hear from women who have made the climb almost, but not quite, to the mountaintop.

I interviewed a dozen high-level women from different federal agencies, all prospective candidates for the Senior Executive Service. Their salaries are reflective of their status.

Only one, a single woman, under age thirty-five, in the work force for ten years, earns slightly less than $40,000 a year. Salaries for all of the others range from $45,000 to $55,000. Their length of federal employment averages twenty years. The shortest tenure is ten years; the longest, forty. All but two are married; one is a widow. Except for one who had stayed in the same agency for twenty-nine years, all the others have changed jobs a minimum of four times and a maximum of ten. They are employed in federal agencies ranging in size from 1,200 to 84,000 employees.

The group included, among others, attorneys, scientists, computer specialists, administrators, program directors, and personnel officers. As you may rightly assume, all entered in lower grades and many in different occupations.

With this brief profile, let's turn to the substance of the interviews.

To my question, what advice would you give college students considering careers in public service and to other women newly embarked on a career, more than half of the women stated: "Get a MBA degree." To this they also added the following recommendations:

- Prepare for a career in computer sciences. For the next decade, at least, this will be the fastest growing area of employment opportunities.
- Cultivate a mentor.
- Use all your contacts to gain entry to meaningful jobs.
- Learn all you can about an organization before you apply for a job, so you can "talk the language."
- Be aggressive in your job search and do not become discouraged if you are not always greeted with open arms.
- If you are qualified for more than one occupational specialty, prepare a separate resume for each field. Focus on your education, skills, and special abilities.
- Take a summer job with exposure to relevant people in your field of interest.
- Join professional organizations.
- Expect some subtle sex discrimination in the job interview and be prepared to deal with it. Anticipate sexist questions.
- Start developing networks early.
- Look for opportunities to get your foot in the door and aggressively market yourself. Emphasize your accomplishments, things that demonstrate competence, leadership, and adaptability.
- Be willing to take risks. Be flexible. Take a challenging job even though it may not necessarily be in your chosen profession.

As for the occupations where they saw the most promising job prospects, the answers were nearly unanimous: law, science, computers, finance, accounting, engineering, and human resource management.

On the subject of mentors, only two claimed never to have had one. Three had had two (male and female); the others each had had one. Several attributed their success to the advice, counsel, and support of their mentors.

Advancement for women is not without its stumbling blocks. Sexism is a major factor in all areas of employment, in public service as well as private employment. Women's magazines, particularly those slanted toward the businesswoman, are replete with articles describing overt or covert sex discrimination in the marketplace. Dozens of cases alleging sex discriminatory employment practices have been won in the courts, after long and arduous struggles. Dozens more are pending on court dockets. A couple of examples have been cited in earlier chapters of this book.

I asked these women if they had encountered sexism along their career paths. Everyone admitted having faced it to one degree or another. A few of their replies:

- In my first federal job men were very chauvinistic. After a year and a half, I transferred to another position before they could hurt my career.
- The negative attitude toward women in high-level positions is readily apparent. Men doing the identical jobs get promoted. The women are ignored. If the women complain, subtle threats emerge, making it impossible to stay on the job.
- In my earlier career as a teacher there were no women principals. When I entered government, there were no women branch chiefs. On several occasions I was the first woman in a particular job. I "toughed it out" and made people respect me as a professional.
- When I began my career in 1962, all male interviewers were concerned that I might get married and start having babies which, they claimed, would be a deterent to my career aspirations.
- After eighteen years in the work force, I still encounter a negative attitude toward women. I have encountered sexual harassment and unequal pay. In one situation, because of sexual harassment, I succeeded in changing jobs. On other occasions I dealt with sexism by demonstrating competence and ability and often was able to earn respect, albeit grudgingly.
- (From an attorney)—Older male lawyers questioned my abilities. Male judges refused to hire women law clerks.

While none of these women is without the scars inflicted by Victorian male attitudes and behavior, the fact remains they were strong enough, tough enough, determined enough, and ambitious enough to overcome the barriers and rise to the crest of the mountain.

Would they have achieved their current levels of success without mandated enforcement of the equal employment opportunity laws and regulations? Based on previous patterns of practice in the power structure, I am not so sure. Of one thing I am sure: all of these women are eminently qualified for their positions.

As I listened to these women relate, in far greater detail than discussed here, the trials and tribulations, stresses and strains, and the joys of successes they encountered on the way up, I found myself thinking, "The more things change, the more they remain the same." I began to reflect on my own experiences in public service.

When my career began in earnest in the 1940s, I had never heard the terms "sex discrimination," "male chauvinism," or "sexual harassment." It wasn't until the early 1960s when Betty Friedan's *The Feminine Mystique* became a best seller and the Civil Rights Act of 1964 drew attention to various forms of discrimination that women became consciously aware of the stereotypical roles to which men had relegated them since time immemorial, especially in the business world.

Having lived in a southern city in the 1940s, I recall when the Commanding Officer of a newly established Air Force Base to which I had been referred for the civilian personnel chief's position, interviewed me. He said: "Gee, I really need a man for this job. But, with all the men off to war, I guess I just may have to settle for 'a girl.' "

Though I said nothing, I was dismayed at being called "a girl." But for the wrong reason. I thought it was because I was so young.

At the conclusion of our interview he said he had several more people to see and would get back to me. I never expected to hear from him again. Several days later he called me to come back for another interview. I went. It was very brief. He said, "You don't have much government experience, but somehow you look so professional, I decided to take a chance on you."

As I left the base and drove back twenty miles to my job, his words kept coming back to me, ". . . you look so professional."

I was pleased, of course, at getting the job but puzzled by the remark. Back at my office, I glanced at myself in the mirrored closet door, and then it struck me. Some years earlier I had seen a movie in which Rosalind Russell portrayed a woman executive. Instantly she became my role model. Perhaps because of my latent ambition to become an executive woman, I began to emulate her style of dress—conservative business suits, coordinated accessories, including hats and gloves. It became such an integral part of me that I soon forgot why I had chosen that type of wardrobe. To this day, except for the hat, I still gravitate toward that type of costume. Subconsciously, perhaps, I thought it might make me more acceptable as a professional and enhance opportunities for advancement. Apparently it worked, at least in this instance.

I hired an all-female staff and for the nearly four years I worked on that base, we were always referred to as "the girls in personnel." Ironically, all but one of "the girls" was married, and one had a ten-year old son. But we were tagged.

About two years later the commanding officer was transferred to another base. Before leaving, he called me to his office to say goodbye. Reminiscing, he told me his concerns and misgivings about hiring a girl as personnel chief had long since been laid to rest. "You've done as good a job as any man could do," he said. "All the officers have told me what an efficient operation you and your girls are running."

I accepted the "compliment" graciously. But walking back to my office, I kept wondering why men should be surprised at women's competence. At the time I didn't recognize a sexist attitude for what it was. I had never heard the term nor a definition of sexism.

As far back as I can remember, my father would tell my sister and me, over and over, that we must make our lives worthwhile. Anything we wanted to do, we could if we'd put our minds to it. I assumed all men felt the same way.

On a different job, in a northern city a few years later, I was boarding a train for a routine assignment to one of our program offices when I heard someone call my name. I turned to find the director of my regional headquarters a few paces behind me. He was heading for a tour of several of our program offices in the same New England area. After exchanging pleasantries, he asked if I would join him for dinner in the dining car. I thought that was a nice gesture and gladly accepted. Throughout dinner we engaged in serious conversation about our region's programs, problems, plans, and so on. We had been talking "shop" for well over an hour, when, out of the blue, as we were sipping a second cup of coffee, he asked if my train accommodations were satisfactory. I had made that trip so many times, I thought it was a silly question. But I answered that they were as good as one could expect on a train. Then his facial expression changed from the serious, businesslike regional director to that of a lecherous old man (he was old enough to be my father), and with a "come hither" look in his eye, he said, "I have a roomette which is far more comfortable and private. Why don't you join me there?"

Frankly, I was so stunned by this sudden turnabout, I just stared at him unbelievingly. I couldn't think of a suitable rebuff. Finally, I said, "I'm a respectable married woman and plan to keep it that way."

He laughed and said, "Gosh, you are a naive kid."

That ended our conversation. I signaled the waiter, paid my check, excused myself, and went back to my car, fuming all the way.

The next morning, standing on the station platform, waiting to be picked up by our local office manager, he walked over and said sneeringly, "I hope you slept well."

"I hope you did too," I replied without so much as a smile.

Arriving at our destination, I went about my business and didn't see him again until late afternoon when our paths crossed in a hallway as he was heading out for a car to drive him to another of our offices. I started to pass him without comment when he put his hand on my arm and stopped me, saying, "Forget about what I said on the train last night. I didn't mean it, I was only testing you."

Furious, I couldn't find words to express myself. I gave him a cold, icy stare and proceeded about my business.

On returning to our regional headquarters a few days later, I found a note from him on my desk: "See me as soon as you return."

My first thought was that I was about to get a dismissal notice on some trumped-up charge because of my resistance to his advances. With my heart pounding and a resurgence of anger overcoming me, I walked into his office and without so much as a "good morning," said coolly, "You wanted to see me?"

Rocking back and forth on his leather swivel chair, he asked if my trip had been successful. I said it was, in just those two words. After what seemed like an eternity of silence, he asked if I had said anything to anyone about "the train incident."

"What train incident?" I asked, emphasizing the word "incident." Then he sat bolt upright, leaned across his desk on both elbows, and in a threatening voice said, "If you like your job, you will never repeat what I said on the train."

Relieved that I was not about to be fired and too angry to reply, I just stared at him, turned, and walked out, snapping the door sharply behind me.

Do these things still happen? Indeed they do! Nothing has changed throughout the years, except that today we have a label for that kind of behavior—"sexual harassment." Fortunately, now there are laws and regulations for dealing with the offenders.

Be prepared to cope with these problems. Especially if you are a young woman on the way up. They exist. They are real. Keep your eyes on your career goals and do not allow yourself to be intimidated. No woman of substance need sacrifice her integrity or her reputation in her quest for recognition and advancement as a competent professional.

7

Conversations
with Corporate Women

In the spring and fall of 1981, I spent several days interviewing, individually, sixteen women from as many different corporations around the country and asked them to share their views on women in the work force, and particularly on employment and career advancement prospects for the decade of the 1980s.

The companies they represented were a cross section of American business and industry. They varied in size from 500 employees to multi-national corporations with several hundred thousand employees, worldwide.

The women ranged in age from twenty-eight to sixty years, with the majority in their thirties and forties. The older women, fifty to sixty years, were refreshingly vibrant, energetic, and vigorous. When each was asked about retirement plans, the answers were

- Never think about it. Have no plans.

- Expect to work as long as physically able.
- Work is the only way to stay young.
- Working at a job you enjoy is the best medicine in the world.

Their years in the work force averaged twenty-two (the shortest was six years, the longest, forty). Four were vice presidents; two were managers of compensation and benefits programs for large corporations; others were variously titled: public relations officer; personnel officer; employee development director; human resources practices specialist; administrator; industrial relations manager; chief, personnel information research; coordinator, special projects and computer systems analyst.

One woman who had retired less than a year ago from the "corporate jungle," as she put it, after forty years in the business world, had recently started a consulting business of her own. "I've always dreamed of being my own boss," she said, "and age sixty seemed like a good time to start."

I asked each interviewee what she considered the most promising fields for women in the 1980s and beyond. Without exception, the answers included the same recommendation: "the exploding field" of data processing, data systems, and computer applications.

From their personal perspective, based on needs within their own companies and those with whom they do business, there was general consensus that other areas offering greatest opportunities for women were in the fields of finance, accounting, marketing, sales (not retail), engineering, mathematics, science, business administration, human resources management, communications, and economics. One, who was in the field of health care, stated that health care management was an expanding field for women and would become more so, based on the evidence of an aging population. More than 25 million people in the United States are over age sixty-five (one out of nine Americans) and their numbers are growing rapidly.

Several of the older women who began their careers as secretaries and typists said they never would have broken out of the stereotyped mold and reached their present status had they not, on their own initiative and on their own time and expense, gone back to colleges and universities for specialized studies and advanced degrees in business administration.

Each was asked to list the principal factors that contributed to her career advancement. Everyone included "hard work" as one. I commented that the data from numerous studies of women's career patterns indicate that hard work alone is no assurance of career advancement. They all agreed, adding that "hard work" meant giving a little more of yourself than what is called for on the job. Never being content just to do your assigned duties, but being ever on the lookout for additional assignments that might carry a higher price tag in the company.

Other answers included the following comments:

- Tenacity on my part and education. By education, I mean taking courses related to the work of my company.
- Developing human relations skills. Knowing how to deal with people to motivate them to be more productive.
- Finding a mentor. Preferably someone in the company who takes an interest in my career development and who is in a position to exert influence.
- Being in the right place at the right time—and knowing it.
- Keeping abreast of the technical advances within the company.
- Having a network of people in the company who know me and my work and are supportive of my ambition.
- Having a role model. In my case it was my assertive, dynamic mother who instilled in me the need to be risk oriented, results oriented, and challenge oriented.
- Previous managers were good coaches. They encouraged me to recognize problems and to cope with them before they became unmanageable.
- Gaining managerial and leadership skill through involvement with professional organizations.
- Refusing to give up even when it appeared that opportunities would not be forthcoming.
- Faith in myself and in the belief that somewhere out there were people who could and would help me, and then setting out to find them.
- Having a supportive home and family life.
- Never hesitating to ask for help and advice.
- Speaking up for myself when appropriate.
- Personal motivation to make maximum utilization of my skills.
- Confidence in my abilities and determination to "make it."
- Having the ability to develop good peer relationships; working well with groups; having a sense of propriety—knowing when to take a leadership profile and when to become part of the group process.

Without exception, education was stressed as a major contributing factor to their success, as well as keeping up with changing technologies and "learning new skills."

Many of the companies included in this survey actually paid tuition for a number of these women to get advanced degrees or to take specialized courses and to participate in conferences sponsored by professional organizations.

Many of the women admitted that this corporate "generosity" could be attributed to the obligation to meet legal requirements for equal opportunity and affirmative action. It made the company "look good" when reporting to the government what steps it had taken to provide opportunities for women and minorities to advance.

More than half of the women were married and had children. A few had grandchildren. One woman raised five children, mostly on her own, after a divorce, while working and taking courses to further her career potential. She is the classic example of Aldous Huxley's thesis concerning "the natural superiority of women."

Others among the group were divorced, widowed, or single. All were active in at least one professional organization. They viewed their careers as an integral part of their lives and would have it no other way.

Yet not one of them was content to accept the status quo. They were always on the lookout for better opportunities to advance their careers. One person had only two job changes in a long career. The rest made between four and eight moves—always moving up a step with each change.

Though all expressed loyalty to their employers, they were well aware that the "corporate climate" in many companies is not to let women get too close to the top where they might compete with men on the way up. So, being astute career women, they always kept their options open and their eyes on the door of opportunity, never hesitating to walk through when it opened—sometimes giving it a shove on their own. That's how they explained the number of job changes.

Their salaries ranged from $20,000 to $50,000 per year. Noting their years of experience, education, and levels of responsibility. I saw it as obvious that had they been men, their salaries would be substantially higher. Statistics abound to substantiate that fact.

The prevailing attitude within the executive suites of the corporate world (and in federal government as well) is that women, especially if they have spouses, "don't need as much money as men." Conversely, men need higher pay to support families. This is an archaic myth in these times, especially in view of the data on the number of women who are heads of households. Yet it is one that is hard to dispel.

Perhaps, as women become more assertive in their quest for greener pastures, the message will register with management that to retain their best people, irrespective of sex or race, they will have to pay them what they are worth. The cost of replacing and training new staff is more costly in the long run.

"How long," I wondered out loud, "do you think it will take for woman's worth to be recognized in the marketplace?"

Not until more women occupy seats of power and reach out to help other women up the ladder—and it may take a decade or more, was the comment of several. Others thought that the current younger generation of male middle-managers are more likely to support upward mobility for women because they are being brought up to accept it as a way of life. Nevertheless they believed it would take a decade.

Some expressed the need to encourage more women to file law suits to ensure equal pay for work of comparable value, citing as an example the fact that the Government of the State of New York pays women office workers $7,195 per annum, while male parking attendants are paid $8,825. The matter of "comparable worth" will be one of the key issues for the next several years.

The reasons for general skepticism boiled down to a realization, based on their respective experiences, that most men over forty-five, especially if they are in management positions, are so steeped in traditional attitudes toward women as to believe that chivalry is what most women want. They cannot accept the obvious—women in the work force want the same things men do—recognition, prestige, power, and money. They still believe a pat on the head and saying "You did a good job, honey," will satisfy most women. Maybe it did twenty-five years ago, but not today. Women who are as well, if not better, educated as men and who have prepared for a career in a professional or technical field want to be accepted for their abilities and not their sex. And that is as it should be.

"Let them shower their paternalism on their children, not on me," stated one up-and-coming woman. "I want the same pay as my male peers—which I'm not getting," she continued, "and I want the same opportunities for advancement."

"When men with less seniority in the company get promoted and I'm told, with a benign smile, that my day will come, that's when I start looking around for another job." So spoke a thirty-five-year-old woman manager who began her career fourteen years ago at a salary of $13,000. Today, after four job changes, the most recent only a few months ago, she is earning $30,000 and is on her way up in a company run by a group of young (age thirty-five to forty-five) male executives whose positive attitude and respect for professional women shows promise for the future.

"When you decided it was time to make a career change, how did you go about it?" I asked several women who had made such changes within the past five years.

All said they had used various "networks," starting with a professional organization in which many other members were in similar or related occupations. Their colleagues were quick to respond and through their recommendations, two of the women found better jobs within six months of beginning the search. For the others it was through different sources: a former faculty advisor who had been a consultant to a major corporation recommended her for employment; friends in other companies who brought the applicants' resumes to the attention of hiring officials, adding their own strong personal endorsement along the way. Only one got her current position through a newspaper advertisement—which she didn't see, but a colleague, knowing of her desire for a better job, brought to her attention.

"Is the work you are now doing in any way related to your college training?" I asked. For most, the answer was "no." Several began their careers as secretaries or typists; others as elementary school teachers; some as bookkeepers; a couple as personnel assistants in fairly large personnel offices; one was a nurse; another a purchasing agent for a government agency.

I found that the women over forty years of age who had been in the work force for twenty or more years started for the most part as typists or stenographers, the only jobs readily available to women at that time, regardless of level of education. Today, professionally trained women still are very often asked if they can type. The general advice is to say "no." Here's a classic case:

A friend of mine, with a Masters degree in political science, had been hired by the administrative assistant to a Congressman to work as a research assistant and speechwriter. Late one afternoon, after preparing material for a speech for the Congressman, she found that all the secretaries had gone for the day. Knowing her boss was scheduled to give the speech the next day, she decided to type it herself.

Around 8 P.M., after pounding away at the typewriter for several hours, the Congressman walked into the office. Surprised at seeing her there, he asked what she was doing in the office so late. When she told him she was typing his speech for the next day, he said, "Oh, I didn't know you could type. That's good. I wish you'd give the secretaries a hand so they can catch up on the backlog of mail," and proceeded to head for his office.

Needless to say, she was furious. Not only because he didn't have the graciousness to thank her for making this special effort on his behalf, but for failing to recognize her as a professional and putting greater value on her ability to type.

She stood up, leaving the unfinished speech in the typewriter, and said, "If typing skills are all you are interested in, perhaps you'd better get another secretary and I'd better start looking for another job where my knowledge and abilities will be recognized for what they are worth. I'll leave the speech for a secretary to type in the morning. I'm sure she will do a better job than I."

Now, Congressmen are accustomed to being stroked, not criticized, especially by their own staffs. He stood with his hand on the door of his office, staring at her as she picked up her purse and coat and rushed toward the door.

"Wait a minute," he called out. "Forgive me. I guess I'm still of the old school—I'm used to 'girls' in the office being secretaries. I never had one who wrote my speeches before."

Feeling herself on the verge of exploding after that inane remark, she said, "I'll pick up my personal belongings in the morning," and stalked out.

Helen arrived at the office early the next morning with a big shopping bag under her arm, intending to gather up her personal items and head for the Congressional employment office. As she approached her desk, tucked away in a back corner of a typically overcrowded Congressional staff office, she found a bouquet of flowers in an attractive vase sitting squarely in the middle with a note saying, "To an outstanding speechwriter whose services are indispensable. Please, please don't leave. Accept my apologies."

Uncharacteristically, the Congressman had apparently arrived very early that morning. "I guess he wanted to get here before I did, to put the flowers on my desk," Helen said.

She headed toward his office to thank him. He stood up when she walked in, "with an expression on his face like that of a puppy who had just messed up the carpet. He looked so pathetic, I decided to give him another chance and stay on the job," Helen said.

They shook hands. She thanked him for the flowers and went back to her desk. Plucking the speech from a typewriter, she gave it to a secretary to finish and went to resume her assigned tasks.

When she told me this story, I asked if his attitude had changed since that episode. She said, "Well, at least he doesn't refer to us as 'the girls' any more. But I'm not ready to call him a feminist."

The corporations represented by my interviewees are subject to the provisions of the Equal Employment Opportunity Act of 1972, which, among other things, requires them to have published Affirmative Action Plans designed to bring women and minorities into the mainstream of the work force. So I asked about their respective companies' programs. All acknowledged that written plans were available. However, as to their effectiveness, the replies were less than gratifying. Here are some of the comments:

- Yes, we have a plan, but no one pays attention to it. It's here in case of a government inspection.
- I wrote my company plan and it's a good one. But instead of assigning me or another staff person to administer it, they brought in a personal friend of the company president whose primary function was to see that no employees file complaints and get us in trouble.
- One good feature of our program is that it provides training in management skills for women. However, only three women occupy senior management positions, compared with several hundred men. The attitude in the organization toward women in high-level positions is negative. "Takes time," management claims. "Women are not yet qualified for major responsibilities." The company policy is to promote from within. Few are hired from outside. Since most of those in line for advancement are men, women have little chance.
- Sure, we have a plan. But with no support from top and middle management, it's just so much paper. (Several replies were along the same line.)
- Our plan provides excellent opportunities for women to get into well-paying, nontraditional occupations in the manufacture of hardware products, but little for professional women.
- For nonprofessional positions, our plan is effective. But it is inoperative when it comes to recruiting women with engineering and scientific degrees. As evidence, only about 1 percent of professional and technical employees are women in a company with more that 300,000 employees worldwide.

These replies are typical of many corporations, according to other women I have interviewed. Many have told me that management still dodges behind the allegation that "qualified" women are not available. They are not willing to make the effort to find them. Nor are they willing to make a firm commitment to affirmative action. They view the program as just another government infringement on their business practices.

In defense of "the establishment," not all companies and corporations in America deserve to be tarred and feathered for failure to implement affirmative action plans. There are some progressive organizations that continue to make a sincere effort to hire, train, and promote women and minorities. The results have been profitable for the companies as well as for the communities in which they operate. By providing more jobs for more people, more expendable income is generated to enrich the coffers of other local businesses.

I cannot leave this chapter without voicing a deep concern for employment prospects for women in the early 1980s.

The Reagan administration continues to demonstrate a bias against affirmative action. Encouraged by this fact, a senator from the State of Utah, with the support of several of his colleagues, proposed legislation that in effect would dismantle existing affirmative action requirements in the private and public sectors. If successful, and with the present conservative Congress, particularly the Senate, it well might happen. Opportunities for women to advance in the work force will be set back to ground zero.

Women must be aware of the action taken by legislators, at the national as well as local levels, that could affect the future course of their lives, professionally as well as personally. It is not enough to sit back and sigh. It is vital that elected representatives be made aware of your concerns by a vigorous campaign of letter writing and telephone calls to prevent a return to the nineteenth-century attitude toward the role of women in our society.

It is particularly disconcerting at this time when the job market is in the doldrums, with unemployment at the highest level since World War II. In the summer of 1982, Northwestern University's Endicott Report (a leading national indicator of job market trends) found a decrease of five to twenty percent in job offers to college graduates. This was confirmed by the Bureau of Labor Statistics, Occupational Outlook Quarterly, Fall 1982, which reported the findings of the College Placement Council that job offers to college graduates had dropped from 62,835 in 1981 to 51,290 in 1982. One reason, it claimed, was that many employers postponed hiring decisions and others cut back on recruiting trips.

The economic forecast is for a substantial increase in employment by the end of the decade, mainly in highly specialized, technical fields such as engineering and the computer sciences, particularly systems analysts.

But will the doors be open equally to women? That's the big question.

The Scientific Manpower Commission' October 1982 MANPOWER COMMENTS reports the results of an interview by Deutsch, Shea & Evans, Inc. with a panel of twenty-five corporate employment experts as to the reasons why so few American women are engineers, technicians or employed in technically-related jobs: "Poor communication by business and schools" is cited as a basic reason. "Contributing factors are cultural conditioning which results in few women considering such careers, and hiring discrimination against women applying for such jobs."

With diminished emphasis on affirmative action, women will have to scramble for a branch on the money tree. To compete successfully, they will have to polish their assertive skills, expand their networks, learn the art of negotiating salaries, and take advantage of the tattered remains of existing law to be assured of equal opportunity in the marketplace. It will not be easy. But from what I have seen of today's young college graduates, I'm convinced they have the stamina, fortitude, and determination to achieve their goals. They should not hesitate to turn to successful women who have achieved their objectives and ask for a helping hand. Most of the women I know are willing and ready to extend that hand.

Climbing the
Management
Ladder

In 1981, about 25 percent of graduates in masters of business administration programs were women. In all likelihood most of these women will inch their way into supervisory and middle-management positions, and, in time, the hardiest of the lot may make it to the executive suites.

Breaking down the barriers and negative attitudes toward women as managers has been aided to some extent by laws and regulations barring sex discrimination. As evidence, the number of women managers and administrators has tripled since 1960. Over three million women now hold such positions.

Yet, in 1982, women occupied only 5 percent of top management positions. Why? Stereotypical attitudes about women's roles, sex bias, and male chauvinism still prevail.

Back in the late 1950s I was interviewed for a position that involved some travel to recruit scientists and engineers for a military installation

162

engaged in research and development activities. The personnel director said my qualifications were outstanding but expressed regret that he couldn't offer me the job because I was a married woman with a child and he was sure that would keep me from meeting the travel requirements. I assured him I would not have applied for the position if I were not free to travel. After hemming and hawing a bit, he explained that I would not be traveling alone. Their agency policy was for the officer in charge of a particular program and his civilian professional counterpart to accompany the personnel specialist on these missions. I replied that on a previous job I often traveled with one or several men on various assignments and never found it a problem.

Fidgeting with a pen on his desk and swiveling back and forth on his chair, he looked me squarely in the eye and said, in a very low tone, that the officer in charge had given him orders not to hire a woman for the position because the men's wives would object to a woman traveling with their husbands. End of interview. No job.

Now, three decades later, I regret to say, many male executives still express the same reservation, though they dare not do so openly because it is forbidden by law to discriminate in employment on the basis of sex.

Despite this underlying current of discrimination, some progress is being made, and women must learn to use their wits and their wisdom if they want to make it into the ranks of management.

There are no rigid guidelines for moving into supervisory or management positions. Based on my own experiences and years of observation, I offer a few insights that might prove helpful in weaving your way into the power structure:

- Begin by looking like you belong there. Clothes and grooming do play a part in the selection process. Your image should convey professionalism and femininity.

- Body language signals something about you. If you walk with an air of confidence, talk with self-assurance, sit without slumping, and look people in the eye when discussing business you will give the impression of someone who knows where she is coming from and where she is going.

- Know your organization well. Not just how it is structured, but what it does. If it is product oriented, learn all you can about its products and its markets. Acquire a working knowledge of the language of the trade or the technical terminology and use it wisely wherever the opportunity arises.

- Observe the management styles that work well in your organization and be able to distinguish them from those that are less successful.

Management styles are as varied as the people who manage. They are a reflection of personalities—egos, if you will—as much as a reflection of professional knowledge and skills.

- Most important, know yourself. Be as objective as possible in recognizing your strengths and your weaknesses. Make a list of both. Concentrate on overcoming the latter. Ask yourself these questions: How effective are my interpersonal communications skills with my peers, subordinates, and supervisors? Am I able to manage people without losing their respect, trust, and confidence? Am I meeting the company's productivity standards with regard to organizing work, delegating tasks, and meeting deadlines? Are people at ease when talking with me? If you have not had enough management experience to evaluate yourself on these factors, think of the answers in terms of your home and family relationships.

- Take stock of where you sit in the corporate structure. Are there many levels of management above you? Are you aware of any planned retirements or transfers that might open avenues for advancement? Don't be bashful about trying to move up, but be subtle and discreet about it. Once the men on the way up learn that you are competing with them for some lofty position, you will find mountains of invisible boulders strewn in your path. Be alert to the signs and avoid the traps.

- Be prepared to take risks, even if it might mean moving to another company.

- If you are turned down for one management position, don't let that be the end of your world. Keep coming back for the next one that opens up.

The corporate affairs director of a major oil company, a woman, once told a group of professional women that, "there's no Hollywood career development in which a company president will walk into an office and 'discover' you. Your career development is really in your hands." She added, "If women really aspire to climbing the corporate ladder they should periodically list their goals, organize their work, learn from others on the job, and develop a good working attitude. You must be able to take constant pressure and to determine who in the organization has power."

Women who have spent many years in non-supervisory jobs, or as assistants to supervisors or managers, often hesitate to seek advancement to supervisory positions. They are fearful of rejection, of being considered "aggressive" or "pushy," while deep down in their hearts they know they are capable of handling the responsibility. Would that I had a dime for every woman in such a position who has had to train her boss for the job as "boss."

Because many jobs, especially in private industry, are filled through the "old-boys' network," women in the company find out about the vacancies after the selection has been made. That's one reason I stress involvement in professional societies. I will share with you a strategy that worked to my advantage, though, admittedly, I had not planned it in the early stages of my affiliation with the organization.

After getting acquainted with some of the people in the local chapter of a national professional organization, I was asked to accept the task of program chair for our monthly meetings. I agreed. The following year I was nominated and elected vice president. The next year I was elected chapter president. By that time I had learned some of the "games" men play in getting their buddies into choice positions. So I decided it was time to develop my own game plan. Several times throughout the year I saw to it that one of my agency's top executives would be invited to be a luncheon speaker. On those occasions in particular, I would invite, as my guest, a photographer and a couple of newspaper reporters who covered such events. Sharing the head table with me, I had an opportunity to engage the speaker in conversation. He got to know me and to observe me in action, in a leadership role. Later I would send the speaker a copy of the photograph taken of him at the meeting along with a note of thanks for his participation. These "getting-to-know-you" occasions opened doors to advancement opportunities for me and for some of my associates.

The litany of "musts" for management positions is long. Here are but a few of the key requirements:

- Have the technical and professional knowledge needed for the particular position you seek.
- Know enough about financial management and accounting to be able to deal with budget preparation and accountability.
- Learn how to bring out the best in people, delegate responsibility, exercise control, implement and monitor programs, and adhere to deadlines.

These are the basic textbook competencies. Much more is expected of a successful manager. Physical stamina, emotional maturity, self-confidence, and assertiveness play an equally important role. It's no secret that for the most part men resent a woman boss and will resist working for one whenever they can.

One time I was interviewing a man for a position on my staff and was about to offer him the job because of his outstanding qualifications and the effective manner in which he presented himself. Then he asked me whom he would be working for. When I told him it would be me, he slapped his palm to his forehead and said, "Ye gods, what would my wife say if she knew I had a lady boss?" I didn't hire him. Some time later I regretted my precipitious act. I should have hired him and let him see that a woman boss was not a threat to life and limb.

Keep in mind that as a woman in management your every action will be carefully observed by the hierarchy. Maintain a friendly relationship with your staff, but don't get too close. They know you are the boss and will expect you to act like one. Be fair in dealing with the people who work for you and take every opportunity to help them develop their own careers. Back them up and support them when the need arises. You will gain their loyalty and respect.

Try to establish a network among other women managers in your organization. Chances are there aren't many of you and you need each other for support and as channels of information.

Remember that the higher you go in a management position the less likely you are to enjoy a nine-to-five routine. You must be prepared to sacrifice much of your home and family life in order to meet the demands of your job. Only you can decide if it's worth it.

The Bottom Line

After years of counseling individual women in planning their careers, guiding them through the hoops of the bureaucracy, watching some falter and fail while many more, confident and determined, marched forward and upward, I came to the conclusion long ago that there really is no single formula for success. The variables in the job market are as unpredictable as life itself. There are no guarantees for finding, keeping, and advancing in a job. A bit of luck—being in the right place at the right time—may help get you started. But where you go from there depends upon many factors.

The old cliche, "Life is what you make it," is a nice generalization, but often it is not entirely within your power to "make it," especially in the business world.

The person who hired you may think you are the greatest. His or her successor may come along—just when you think you are in line for advancement or have been getting good vibes about your future—with ideas for reorganization or replacing you with someone else with whom he or she feels more comfortable or whose performance is more predictable. When that happens, and it often does, it's time to look elsewhere, without tears or tantrums, but with determination to find another niche for yourself.

Personality clashes, office politics, jockeying for power are among the hazards of the workplace.

Knowledge and awareness of these human frailties can protect you to some extent from bruising experiences.

Then of course there are economic considerations. In mid-1982 business failures equaled those of the Great Depression of the early 1930s. Numerous recent bank failures also are reminiscent of the 1930s. Corporate earnings reports hold little promise for improvement in the immediate future.

Reduced federal budgets, mandated by the current administration, have thrown thousands of career civil servants out of government jobs.

The sounds of gloom and doom pervade the atmosphere in business and government.

Yet, pages and pages of "help wanted" advertisements fill the daily newspapers and professional journals. Executive recruiters, "head hunters" as they are known in the trade, continue to search for top-level managers for corporations of every size and description.

The Office of Personnel Management continues to annouce civil service job opportunities throughout the United States, though not in all occupations.

So what do these conflicting signals tell you? The first message is that finding your first job in 1983 may be a bit tough—unless you are in one of the specialized fields in great demand: computer programming, engineering, and systems analysis. The second message is that you must prepare for your career by becoming aware of your assets and liabilities and capitalize on you assets. For starters:

- Be exceptionally well prepared for your chosen profession.
- Focus on the job at hand, but at the same time be alert to the overall needs of your organization.
- Don't concentrate on one narrow area of specialization indefinitely.
- Keep your antenna up—listen to the sounds of movement throughout your company or agency: in business or industry if inventories are high, new orders are low, and corporate earnings statements are in the doldrums, maybe it's time to start discreetly job hunting, especially if there are significant changes in key executives and rumblings about

takeovers and mergers. It behooves you to read some of the business journals to find out what's going on in your company, as well as the company's quarterly and annual report to stockholders. The sources are many. Among them: *The Wall Street Journal, Barron's, Forbes* magazine, *Business Week* and others.

- In government two excellent sources of information are available: *The Federal Times,* which covers in considerable detail the happenings in federal agencies and in the Congress; and the *Federal Employees News Digest,* which summarizes governmental activities affecting federal employees. Both are weekly publications. Keep an eye on what Congress is doing and saying about your agency's appropriation. If funds are being slashed and rumors abound about program cutbacks and reductions in force, begin to explore prospects for jobs in more stable agencies. Admittedly there is little stability in any federal agency during the current Administration except for the Department of Defense. Two agencies to avoid are the Department of Energy and the Department of Education.

- Expand your horizons to keep pace with changing times and changing technologies.

- Set goals and timetables for yourself. Have some clearly defined objectives for specific intervals: Know where you want to be in two years and again in five years. If at the end of two years you do not have a sense of progress, it is time to reexamine the reasons. Perhaps some career counseling with a competent counselor may be in order. Or you may need some reeducation or additional education that will broaden your opportunities to advance. Maybe you need to consider some other discipline for which you could qualify with some specialized training.

- Keep channels of communication open at all levels. If you are fortunate to have a supervisor who is truly committed to the goals of the organization, knows how to deal effectively with people, and is willing to assist staff in fulfilling their career goals, take advantage of it and discuss your future prospects. On the other hand, if your supervisor is a "tiger" or a "nitpicker," you know you will not get very far, so start looking around for a change.

- If you have an MBA or a PhD, don't expect the keys to the executive washroom within the first year or two. But if you don't find yourself on a career path, it's time to take stock.

- Be alert to the signs of jealousy or envy among peers and supervisors who may try to keep you from getting too far too fast—especially true for women. The business world is full of people whose attitude is "If I can't get ahead, neither will he or she." They can create many roadblocks for you in subtle ways. Learn to avoid the pitfalls.

- Cultivate your business colleagues judiciously and selectively.

- Be assertive without being aggressive. Bear in mind the prevailing myth—and a myth it is—that assertive women are considered "pushy." Assertive men, on the other hand, are regarded as "go-getters."
- Don't hide your light under a bushel basket. If you don't demonstrate confidence in your abilities, if you remain passive and reluctant to be a little "pushy," you will be left at the starting gate.
- When you attend a staff meeting, or any other meeting within your organization, with your professional peers and are the only woman present, don't volunteer to take notes or serve the coffee. If you weren't there, the men would manage to get their own coffee. If you are asked to take notes, graciously decline and suggest a secretary be called in, or say you are no more competent at note taking than the others present. Said with a smile and in a gentle voice, you will win the respect of your male peers. You will never be put upon a second time. If you behave as a professional, you will be treated as one. (Call this delicate assertive behavior.)
- Don't bring your personal or family problems to the job and never use such problems as an excuse for failure to accomplish assigned tasks.
- Don't be afraid of responsibility—seek it. Don't wait to be told what to do. Exercise initiative. There's always competition for the next-higher-level position. Make yourself indispensable.
- Believe in yourself. Self-esteem is critical. However, discretion is advised. Don't tread on others' toes. Be aware that the impression you make on peers and subordinates can significantly affect your future career. One of them could become your boss someday.
- Tune in to office politics and learn to play the game.
- Keep abreast of the literature in your field. Subscribe to publications dealing with your area of specialization (or borrow them from libraries).
- Join one or more professional organizations, especially those to which your peers, your boss, or other high-level people belong, to increase your visibility and demonstrate interest in further professional development.
- Join women's networks.
- Learn to take constructive criticism objectively, not emotionally.
- Periodically, at least once a year, reevaluate your job. Make a list of those elements that give you satisfaction and a sense of accomplishment and those that are frustrating and nonrewarding. Decide which of the negative elements you have the power to change, perhaps in consultation with your supervisor, and which you, or, your supervisor are powerless to change. If the latter are excessive, start investigating prospects for a job change within your organization. If that's not feasible, dust off your resume and start job shopping.

Forearmed with these guidelines and with the required knowledge and skills, courage to take some risks, awareness of human behavior, determination, flexibility, willingness to learn, eagerness to achieve, and respect for others' views, the path to a successful career will be that much smoother.

That's the bottom line.

Bibliography

BOOKS

BOLLES, R. N., *What Color is Your Parachute?* Berkeley, Calif.: Ten Speed Press, 1978.

CANNIE, J. K., *The Woman's Guide to Management Success.* Englewood Cliffs, N. J.: Prentice-Hall, Inc., 1979.

HARRAGAN, B. L., *Games Mother Never Taught You.* New York: Rawson Associates Publisher, 1977.

JOSEFOWITZ, N., *Paths to Power.* Reading, Mass.: Addison-Wesley Co., 1980.

KANTER, R. M., *Men and Women of the Corporation.* New York: Basic Books, Inc., 1977.

KENNEDY, M. M., *Office Politics.* New York: Warner Books, 1980.

RUSSELL, A., and P. FITZGIBBONS, *Career and Conflict: A Woman's Guide to Making Life Choices.* Englewood Cliffs, N. J., Prentice-Hall, Inc., 1982.

SARGENT, A. G., *The Androgynous Manager.* New York: AMACOM, 1981.

WELCH, M. S., *Networking.* New York: Harcourt Brace Jovonovich, 1980.

ARTICLES

FITT, L. W., and D. A. NEWTON, "When the Mentor is a Man and the Protege A Woman," *Harvard Business Review,* March-April 1981, pp. 56-60.

ROCHE, G. R., "Much Ado About Mentors," *Harvard Business Review,* January-February 1979, pp. 14-24.

OTHER REFERENCES

Report of the President's Task Force on Women's Rights and Responsibilities, *A Matter of Simple Justice,* Supt. of Documents, Government Printing Office, Washington, D. C., 1970.

Report on the National Commission on the Observance of International Women's Year, . . . *to Form a More Perfect Union,* U. S. Department of State, Washington, D. C., 1976.

Information on the activities of other organizations mentioned in this book may be obtained by writing to

Federally Employed Women (FEW), 1010 Vermont Ave., N.W., Washington, D.C. 20005.

National Organization for Women (NOW), 425 13th St. N.W., Washington, D.C. 2004

National Women's Political Caucus, 1411 K St., N.W., Washington, D.C. 20005.

Women's Equity Action League (WEAL), 805 Fifteenth Street, N.W., Washington, D. C. 20005

Index

182